日本語 NC
NihonGO N

NihonGO NOW! is a beginning-level courseware package that takes a performed-culture approach to learning Japanese. This innovative approach balances the need for an intellectual understanding of structural elements with multiple opportunities to experience the language within its cultural context.

From the outset, learners are presented with samples of authentic language that are context-sensitive and culturally coherent. Instructional time is used primarily to rehearse interactions that learners of Japanese are likely to encounter in the future, whether they involve speaking, listening, writing, or reading.

Level 1 comprises two textbooks with accompanying activity books. These four books in combination with audio files allow instructors to adapt a beginning-level course, such as the first year of college Japanese, to their students' needs. They focus on language and modeled behavior, providing opportunities for learners to acquire language through performance templates. Online resources provide additional support for both students and instructors. Audio files, videos, supplementary exercises, and a teachers' manual are available at www.routledge.com/9781138304147.

NihonGO NOW! Level 1 Volume 2 Activity Book provides a wealth of communicative exercises and assessment tools for students working through the second semester of the *NihonGO NOW!* course.

Mari Noda is Professor of Japanese at The Ohio State University.

Patricia J. Wetzel is Emerita Professor of Japanese at Portland State University.

Ginger Marcus is Professor of the Practice of Japanese Language at Washington University in St. Louis.

Stephen D. Luft is Lecturer of Japanese at the University of Pittsburgh.

Shinsuke Tsuchiya is Assistant Professor of Japanese at Brigham Young University.

Masayuki Itomitsu is Associate Professor of Japanese at Linfield College.

日本語 NOW!
NihonGO NOW!

Performing Japanese Culture
Level 1 Volume 2
Activity Book

Mari Noda, Patricia J. Wetzel, Ginger Marcus,
Stephen D. Luft, Shinsuke Tsuchiya,
and Masayuki Itomitsu

Routledge
Taylor & Francis Group
LONDON AND NEW YORK

First published 2021
by Routledge
2 Park Square, Milton Park, Abingdon, Oxon OX14 4RN

and by Routledge
52 Vanderbilt Avenue, New York, NY 10017

Routledge is an imprint of the Taylor & Francis Group, an informa business

British Library Cataloguing-in-Publication Data
A catalogue record for this book is available from the British Library

Library of Congress Cataloging-in-Publication Data
Names: Noda, Mari, author.
Title: Nihongo now! : performing Japanese culture / Mari Noda, Patricia J. Wetzel, Ginger Marcus, Stephen D. Luft, Shinsuke Tsuchiya, Masayuki Itomitsu.
Description: New York : Routledge, 2020. | Includes bibliographical references. | Contents: Level 1, volume 1. Textbook — Level 1, volume 1. Activity book — Level 1, volume 2. Textbook — Level 1, volume 2. Activity book. | In English and Japanese.
Identifiers: LCCN 2020026010 (print) | LCCN 2020026011 (ebook) | ISBN 9780367509279 (level 1, volume 1 ; set ; hardback) | ISBN 9780367508494 (level 1, volume 1 ; set ; paperback) | ISBN 9781138304123 (level 1, volume 1 ; textbook ; hardback) | ISBN 9781138304147 (level 1, volume 1 ; textbook ; paperback) | ISBN 9781138304277 (level 1, volume 1 ; activity book ; hardback) | ISBN 9781138304314 (level 1, volume 1 ; activity book ; paperback) | ISBN 9780367509309 (level 1, volume 2 ; set ; hardback) | ISBN 9780367508531 (level 1, volume 2 ; set ; paperback) | ISBN 9780367483241 (level 1, volume 2 ; textbook ; hardback) | ISBN 9780367483210 (level 1, volume 2 ; textbook ; paperback) | ISBN 9780367483494 (level 1, volume 2 ; activity book ; hardback) | ISBN 9780367483364 (level 1, volume 2 ; activity book ; paperback) | ISBN 9780203730249 (level 1, volume 1 ; ebook) | ISBN 9780203730362 (level 1, volume 1 ; ebook) | ISBN 9781003051855 (level 1, volume 1 ; ebook) | ISBN 9781003039334 (level 1, volume 2 ; ebook) | ISBN 9781003039471 (level 1, volume 2 ; ebook) | ISBN 9781003051879 (level 1, volume 2 ; ebook)
Subjects: LCSH: Japanese language—Textbooks for foreign speakers—English. | Japanese language—Study and teaching—English speakers.
Classification: LCC PL539.5.E5 N554 2020 (print) | LCC PL539.5.E5 (ebook) | DDC 495.682/421—dc23
LC record available at https://lccn.loc.gov/2020026010
LC ebook record available at https://lccn.loc.gov/2020026011

ISBN: 978-0-367-48349-4 (hbk)
ISBN: 978-0-367-48336-4 (pbk)
ISBN: 978-1-003-03947-1 (ebk)

Typeset in Times New Roman
by Apex CoVantage, LLC

Visit the eResources: www.routledge.com/9781138304147

Contents

第 7 幕
Act 7

びっくりしました。

I was surprised.

◆ Scene 7-1 練習 Practice

理解練習 Comprehension practice

7-1-1C Which one is better?

Listen to Yamada-san express her opinions on various matters, then select the quality being compared from the options below and mark the one that she says has more of that quality.

a. Convenient	b. Spacious	c. Hot	d. Available	e. Dark
f. New	g. Big	h. Easy	i. Inexpensive	j. Lonely

Ex. 1. ___a___	☐ Train	☒ Bus
Ex. 2. ___h___	☒ Korean	☐ German
3. ________	☐ This week	☐ Next week
4. ________	☐ This one	☐ That one over there
5. ________	☐ Today	☐ Tomorrow
6. ________	☐ Last year	☐ This year
7. ________	☐ This place	☐ That other place
8. ________	☐ Mom	☐ Dad

実演練習 Performance practice

7-1-2P Suggesting otherwise (BTS 1)

Your friend, Mizuno-san, seems to think that another friend, Ito-san, is not very proactive. Gently suggest that Ito-san probably does all the things that Mizuno-san thinks she doesn't.

Ex. 1.

Mizuno-san	伊藤さんは復習しないから……。	Ito-san doesn't review them, so . . .
You	え?いや、復習するでしょう。	What? No, she probably does review them.

Ex. 2.

Mizuno-san	伊藤さんは何も言わないから……。	Ito-san doesn't say anything, so . . .
You	え?いや、言うでしょう。	What? No, she probably does say something.

7-1-3P Reassuring that you are adjusting well (BTS 2)

You've just begun to work at a new company. Taguchi-san, your new colleague, is concerned about various aspects of your new environment. Reassure her that you have gotten used to them.

Ex. 1.

Taguchi-san	寒いでしょう、この部屋。大丈夫?	It's cold—this room. Are you all right?
You	まあ、この部屋の寒さにはもう慣れましたから。	Well, I've already gotten used to the cold temperature in this room, so . . .

Ex. 2.

Taguchi-san	アパートは便利だけど、ちょっと狭いですか?	The apartment is convenient, but is it a bit small?
You	まあ、アパートの狭さにはもう慣れましたから。	Well, I've already gotten used to the smallness of the apartment, so . . .

7-1-4P Specifying the extent with a comparison (Act 6 BTS 24)

When Tamura-san, a co-worker, asks you a question, provide a comparison to show the extent to which she would be correct. The item for your comparison is provided below.

Ex. 1.

Tamura-san	難しいですか?日本語。	Is it difficult? Japanese, I mean.
You	まあ、フランス語よりは難しいですけどね。	Well, it's harder than French.

Ex. 2.

Tamura-san	忙しいですか?今週。	Are you busy? This week, I mean.
You	まあ、先週よりは忙しいですけどね。	Well, I'm busier than last week.

Ex. 1. French
Ex. 2. Last week
3. Here
4. The one on the second floor
5. The work from yesterday
6. Last month
7. The apartment below
8. Kimura-san's
9. The one on the first floor

7-1 腕試し Tryout

1. Ask some acquaintances who recently moved somewhere if they've gotten used to things yet.
2. Ask a couple of your friends what type of things/times/places they find stressful, pleasing, sad, easy to do, they want to do, etc. You may not understand all of what they say in their response. Try to pick one word that catches your attention and ask what it means (recall Act 3 Scene 1).
3. Find out from your Japanese friends and/or associates what sorts of things come to mind when they hear descriptive words such as うれしい, さびしい, etc. You can do this by asking, for example, うれしいことってどんなことですか?

◆ Scene 7-2 練習 Practice

理解練習 Comprehension practice

7-2-1C What's going on? (BTS 4)

You will hear your friend Shoma say something in two ways. For each utterance, identify which one of the two descriptions corresponds to Shoma's situation.

例 1-1	a / ⓑ	a. Shoma didn't expect the air conditioner to be on, but when he entered the room, it was actually quite cool.
例 1-2	ⓐ / b	b. Shoma is walking somewhere with his supervisor and finds the weather to be rather cool.
2-1	c / d	c. Shoma and his project partner need a reference book. Shoma thinks they can borrow it from the library and is checking if his partner agrees.
2-2	c / d	d. Shoma's friend needs a reference book for her project. When Shoma suggested she buy one online, she said she's not going to buy it.
3-1	d / f	e. Shoma just finished with his shift at his part-time job. He wants to tell his co-worker that he will be back again tomorrow.
3-2	d / f	f. At the end of his shift at his part-time job, Shoma's co-worker says, "See you in a week." Shoma will be back again tomorrow.
4-1	g / h	g. Shoma's friend just mentioned how he was talking to Tanaka-san the other day. Shoma didn't know that he actually knew Tanaka-san.
4-2	g / h	h. Shoma is about to say something about Tanaka-san, and is wondering if his friend knows Tanaka-san or not.
5-1	i / j	i. Shoma's classmate invites him out to dinner, but the entire class has been invited to a party tomorrow.
5-2	i / j	j. There is a party tomorrow for all international students and Shoma decided to invite a friend to attend it.

実演練習 Performance practice

7-2-2P Showing agreement with amplification (BTS 4)

When Kato-san, your senior colleague, suggests an alternative, agree by pointing out its benefit.

Ex. 1.

Kato-san	外は寒くても、中は?	Even if it's cold outside, what about the inside?
You	そう、そう。中は暖かいんですよね。	Right, right. Inside, it's warm, isn't it!

Ex. 2.

Kato-san	会社の場所は不便でも、食堂は?	Even if the company location is inconvenient, what about the dining hall?
You	そう、そう。食堂は便利なんですよね。	Right, right. The dining hall is convenient, isn't it!

7-2-3P Confirming the order of business (BTS 4, 5)

You and your senior colleague, Kato-san, are out on business together. He suggests that you first do something before returning to the office. Confirm that you will perform that task, then go back.

Ex. 1.

Kato-san	早く帰りたいでしょうけど、先にこれやりましょう。	You are probably eager to go return to the office, but let's first do this.
You	これやって、それから帰るんですね。了解です。	So we do this, then go home, right? I got it.

Ex. 2.

Kato-san	早く帰りたいでしょうけど、先に隣に寄りましょう。	You are probably eager to return to the office, but let's first stop next door.
You	隣に寄って、それから帰るんですね。了解です。	So we stop next door, then go home, right? I got it.

7-2-4P Explaining that you want to, but . . . (BTS 4)

When your colleague, Fujiwara-san, confirms that you're not doing something, explain that you want to, and then add why you won't, based on the information provided.

Ex. 1.

Fujiwara-san	新しいの買わないんですか。	You're not going to buy a new one?
You	買いたいんですけど、ちょっと高いんです。	I want to, but it's a little expensive.

Ex. 2.

Fujiwara-san	行かないんですか？	You're not going?
You	行きたいんですけど、木村さんがもう行っているんです。	I want to, but Kimura-san has already gone (there).

Ex. 1. It's a little expensive.
Ex. 2. Kimura-san has already gone (there).
3. The work is not yet finished.
4. You'll be having lunch shortly.
5. Tomorrow is your day off.
6. You don't have a camera.
7. You have work.
8. You're a little sick.
9. You haven't yet consulted with the division chief.

7-2 腕試し Tryout

1. Ask someone about their upcoming trip or an event. Find out if they are looking forward to it, and ask questions about the details of the trip or the event.
2. Find out more about someone's family, such as the size of their family, if they have any brothers or sisters, and where family members live. Be sensitive to vague answers that could suggest they would like to keep family matters more private.

◆ Scene 7-3 練習 Practice

理解練習 Comprehension practice

7-3-1C Hearsay or not? (BTS 9)

Listen to the conversation. If one of the speakers is reporting information s/he heard from someone else, mark "hearsay"; if not, mark "not hearsay."

Ex. 1.	☒ Hearsay	☐ Not hearsay
Ex. 2.	☐ Hearsay	☒ Not hearsay
3.	☐ Hearsay	☐ Not hearsay
4.	☐ Hearsay	☐ Not hearsay
5.	☐ Hearsay	☐ Not hearsay
6.	☐ Hearsay	☐ Not hearsay
7.	☐ Hearsay	☐ Not hearsay
8.	☐ Hearsay	☐ Not hearsay
9.	☐ Hearsay	☐ Not hearsay
10.	☐ Hearsay	☐ Not hearsay

実演練習 Performance practice

7-3-2P Relaying information to a relevant person (BTS 9, 8)

Relay the information you hear on the phone to your colleague, Yamada-san.

Ex. 1.

Caller	あ、すみません。下の売店ですが、山田さんの財布がございました。	Oh, sorry to bother you. This is the kiosk downstairs calling. Yamada-san's wallet was found here.
You (to Yamada-san)	下の売店から電話で、山田さんの財布があったって。	It's a call from the kiosk downstairs, and they found your wallet.

Ex. 2.

Takeda-san	あ、すみません。山田の姉ですが、午後そちらに伺いますから。	Oh, sorry to bother you. This is Yamada's older sister, but I'll be visiting your office this afternoon, so . . .

You (to Yamada-san)	お姉さんから電話で、午後こちらにいらっしゃるって。	It's a call from your older sister, and she is coming here this afternoon.

7-3-3P Showing surprise (BTS 4, 6, 8, 9)

You and Takeda-san, a member of your community group, are sharing some surprising news about someone in your family. Express your surprise about what you've heard. For this practice, assume that you have a big family.

Ex. 1.

Takeda-san	へえ、お姉さんも全部泳いだんですか？	Wow, your older sister swam the whole thing, too?
You	そうなんです。姉も泳いだと聞いて、私もびっくりしました。	Indeed! Hearing that my older sister swam, too, I was also surprised.

Ex. 2.

Takeda-san	へえ、お母さんも富士山に登ったんですか？	Wow, your mother climbed Mt. Fuji, too?
You	そうなんです。母も登ったと聞いて、私もびっくりしました。	Indeed! Hearing that my mother climbed, too, I was also surprised.

7-3-4P Two-part explanations (BTS 4, 8)

When Hasegawa-san asks you what happened, provide some background information before saying what went wrong, based on the information given.

Ex. 1.

Hasegawa-san	どうしたんですか。	What happened?
You	部長に相談したんですけど、ダメだって言ったんです。	I consulted the division chief, but she said no.

Ex. 2.

Hasegawa-san	どうしたんですか。	What happened?
You	八時に家を出たんですけど、バスが遅れたんです。	I left home at 8 o'clock, but the bus was late.

	Background information	**What went wrong**
Ex. 1.	You consulted the division chief.	She said no.
Ex. 2.	You left home at 8 o'clock.	The bus was late.
3.	You waited a long time.	He didn't come.
4.	You did the homework.	You didn't understand well.

5.	Nakamura-san said he'd come.	He didn't come.
6.	You dropped by the office.	Kanda-san (the person you were looking for) wasn't there.
7.	You ordered tea.	It hasn't come (lit. it doesn't come).
8.	You took two days off.	You are still sick.
9.	The weather was good.	Miura-san didn't come.
10.	You read the whole thing.	It's difficult and you don't understand.

7-3 腕試し Tryout

1. Try telling someone about something that one of your family members has done.
2. Relay information by quoting what you have heard to your Japanese colleagues or friends. The content of the information may be in English, Japanese, or whatever language you have heard it in. But frame it appropriately, using ～って言っていました or ～っておっしゃっていました, depending on the source and the relationship that exists between the source and yourself.

◆ Scene 7-4 練習 Practice

理解練習 Comprehension practice

7-4-1C Agree or disagree? (BTS 11, 12)

Listen to the conversation to see if the second (female) speaker is agreeing with the first speaker. If so, mark “agree.” If not, mark “disagree.”

Ex. 1.	☒ Agree	☐ Disagree
Ex. 2.	☐ Agree	☒ Disagree
3.	☐ Agree	☐ Disagree
4.	☐ Agree	☐ Disagree
5.	☐ Agree	☐ Disagree
6.	☐ Agree	☐ Disagree
7.	☐ Agree	☐ Disagree
8.	☐ Agree	☐ Disagree

実演練習 Performance practice

7-4-2P Responding to a show of concern (BTS 11)

When Saito-san, an acquaintance through work, asks about your well-being, report that you are better, thanking her for being concerned.

Ex. 1.

Saito-san	どうですか、ご気分。まだあまり良くないって?	How are you feeling? I hear you’re still not doing well?
You	おかげさまで、もうかなりよくなりました。	Thanks to you and everyone, I’m already feeling much better.

Ex. 2.

Takeda-san	ご病気ですか?元気ないって聞きましたけど……。	Are you ill? I heard that you were feeling worn out.
You	おかげさまで、もうかなり元気になりました。	Thanks to you and everyone, I’m already a lot better.

7-4-3P I don't think so (BTS 12)

When your friend Ai asks you a question about Ichiro-kun, respond that you don't think so, following the pattern.

Ex. 1.

Ai	しなかったかな。	I wonder if he didn't do it.
You	いや、したと思うよ。	No, I think he did it.

Ex. 2.

Ai	来るかな。	I wonder if he's coming.
You	いや、来ないと思うよ。	No, I don't think he's coming.

7-4-4P I've been thinking I'd like to (BTS 12)

When your colleague Murata-san asks you if you will do something, respond by saying that you've been thinking you'd like to.

Ex. 1.

Murata-san	行きますか。	Are you going to go?
You	はい、行きたいと思っています。	Yes, I've been thinking I'd like to go.

Ex. 2.

Murata-san	伺いますか。	Are you going to visit (him)?
You	はい、伺いたいと思っています。	Yes, I've been thinking I'd like to visit (him).

7-4 腕試し Tryout

1. Formally thank someone for something significant that she did for you.
2. Ask someone who's been sick how he is feeling.
3. Express your sympathy to someone who's sick (i.e., tell them to take care).

◆ Scene 7-5 練習 Practice

理解練習 Comprehension practice

7-5-1C Identifying Sentence Modifiers (BTS 14)

In each conversation you will hear a Sentence Modifier, where a Verb modifies a Noun. Match the Verb on the left with the Noun it modifies on the right. You may use an option more than once.

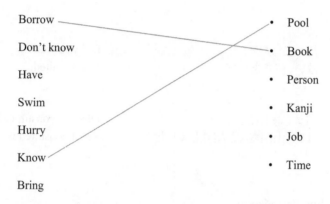

Borrow	• Pool
Don't know	• Book
Have	• Person
Swim	• Kanji
Hurry	• Job
Know	• Time
Bring	

実演練習 Performance practice

7-5-2P Giving permission to a particular group of people (BTS 14)

You are a supervising member of a group. When Matsumoto-san, a group member, tells you something about himself and another group member, acknowledge that you heard and then ask if there is anyone in the group in a similar situation.

Ex. 1.

Matsumoto-san	あのう、僕も井上君も、まだできてないんですが……。	Um, both Inoue-kun and I aren't done yet, but . . .
You	そうですか。まだできてない人、ほかにいますか。	I see. Are there others who aren't done yet?

Ex. 2.		
Matsumoto-san	僕も渡辺君も、帰りたいんですが……。	Both Watanabe-kun and I are going home, but . . .
You	そうですか。帰りたい人、ほかにいますか。	I see. Are there others who are going home?

7-5-3P I did it with Yamada-san (Act 6 BTS 25)

When Sato-san asks if you did an activity, respond based on the entries in your daily planner below, which are from the past two days. If you did the activity with Yamada-san, provide that information when you respond. If you did the activity by yourself, simply respond affirmatively.

Ex. 1.		
Sato-san	待ちました?	Did you wait?
You	はい、待ちましたよ。	Yes, I waited.

Ex. 2.		
Sato-san	相談しました?	Did you consult (with someone)?
You	はい、山田さんと相談しましたよ。	Yes, I consulted with Yamada-san.

7/5
Play tennis with Yamada-san
Buy notebooks
Decide the conference location with Yamada-san
Consult about the conference schedule with Yamada-san
Go running

7/6
Go on a walk
Talk about the report with Yamada-san
Wait for Kimura-san at the train station
Help Kimura-san
Study economics with Yamada-san

7-5-4P Stating how many were involved (Act 6 BTS 25)

Maeda-san, your senior, asks if you did something all by yourself. Correct the misunderstanding by indicating that you did it with one or more friends, as indicated.

Ex. 1. + 

Maeda-san	え?全部一人でやったんですか、これ。すごいなあ。	You did it all by yourself, this? That's amazing!
You	いやいや、友達と、4人でやったんですよ。	No, no. I did it with friends, four of us.

Ex. 2. + 

Maeda-san	ああ、あの映画ね。どうだった?一人で見に行ったの?	Oh, that movie. How was it? Did you go see it by yourself?
You	いやいや、友達と、7人で行ったんですよ。	No, no. I went with friends, seven of us.

3.	4.	5.
+ 	+ 	+ 
6.	**7.**	**8.**
+ 	+ 	+ 

7-5 腕試し Tryout

1. Participate in an activity with a group of people. When decisions are made as a group, participate in the decision-making process, being careful not to be too direct in expressing your own opinion, and being sensitive to the overall wishes of the group.
2. Find out the commuting patterns of your classmates (or a group of your work associates). You can begin by asking who comes by car, by bus, on foot, etc. (車で来る人は?).
3. Poll opinions of your classmates (or a group of work associates) by positing possibilities and asking who thinks in a particular way. For example, introduce the parking situation at your school or work place as a topic (ここのパーキングですが、), then ask if there are people who think it's convenient/inconvenient (便利だと思う人、いますか。不便だと思う人は?)

◆ Scene 7-6 練習 Practice

理解練習 Comprehension practice

7-6-1C What's going on? (BTS 18)

Listen to each statement and select the option that best reflects what the speaker believes.

Ex. 1.	b	Ex. 2.	b	3.	______	4.	______	5.	______
6.	______	7.	______	8.	______	9.	______	10.	______
11.	______	12.	______	13.	______				

Ex. 1. a. He's going.
b. He's not going.

Ex. 2. a. It's my younger brother's.
b. It's not my younger brother's.

3. a. Yamazaki-kun will do the climb.
b. Yamazaki-kun won't do the climb.

4. a. She said she wanted the black one.
b. She didn't say she wanted the black one.

5. a. It is expensive.
b. It's not expensive.

6. a. That person is a teacher.
b. That person is not a teacher.

7. a. He said he'd come tomorrow.
b. He didn't say he'd come tomorrow.

8. a. That person is her husband.
b. That person isn't her husband.

9. a. It's a cheap one.
b. It's not a cheap one.

10. a. She'll bring a lot.
b. She won't bring a lot.

11. a. That place is a factory.
b. That place isn't a factory.

12. a. Yuya-kun will go.
b. Yuya-kun won't go.

13. a. Smith-san is in England.
b. Smith-san is not in England

7-6-2C What's going on? (BTS 17)

Listen to each set of directions and indicate on the diagram how you should get to the destination. Your starting point and the direction you face are indicated with a solid triangle.

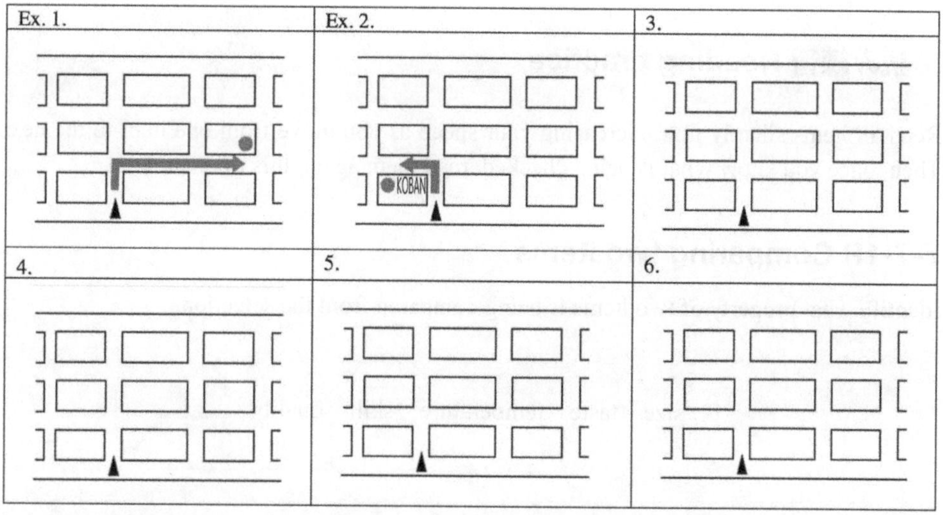

実演練習 Performance practice

7-6-3P Trying to remember what something/somebody is called (BTS 19)

Maeda-san is trying to identify something/someone. Indicate that it's a name you know but can't recall at the moment.

Ex. 1.

Maeda-san	カフェでしょう?	It's a café, right?
You	はい、何とかカフェですけど……。	Yes. It's a café named something or other, but . . .

Ex. 2.

Maeda -san	定食でしょう?	It's a set meal, right?
You	はい、何とか定食ですけど……。	Yes. It's a set meal called something or other, but . . .

7-6 腕試し Tryout

1. Give someone directions to a location.
2. Ask someone for directions to a location. Be sure to repeat back what she tells you so that she knows you've understood correctly.

◆ Scene 7-7 練習 Practice

読み練習 Reading practice

Read all items silently first, increasing your speed as you move from one item to the next. Then, once you know what is being checked, read them again, this time out loud.

7-7-1R Comparing two items

Identify what property of two items is being compared from the selection.

size	taste	temperature	skill	quality

Ex. 1. フィレンツェよりヴェネチアのほうがいいと思います。 quality

Ex. 2. デラウェアよりインディアナのほうが大きいと思います。 size

3. ニュージャージーよりウィスコンシンのほうが寒いと思います。 ______

4. ウィルソンさんよりコンウェイさんのほうが英語が上手だと思います。 ______

5. クォーターパウンダーよりフィレオフィッシュのほうがおいしいと思います。 ______

7-7-2R Expressing surprise

Identify the source of surprise from the selection in each of the statements.

a. someone's home state	b. formality of an event	c. someone's educational background
d. lack of communication	e. dating frequency	f. where the drink was purchased

Ex. 1. え、あしたもデートするんですか。 e

Ex. 2. え、メールをチェックしないんですか。 d

3. え、あのパーティーはフォーマルなんですか。 ______

4. え、マーティネスさんはスタンフォードなんですか。 ______
5. え、このカフェオレはファミリーマートのなんですか。 ______
6. え、ウォーカーさんはフィラデルフィアからなんですか。 ______

◆ Scene 7-8 練習 Practice

読み練習 Reading practice

7-8-1R Coming or going?

Identify the appropriate motion verb that fits in each blank. You may use each option once.

Ex. 1.	セントルイスにはもう___a___よ。すごくきれいだった!	a. 行った
Ex. 2.	来月、うちのピアノリサイタルがありますが、___g___か。	b. 行かない
3.	うちのサークルにはおととい______んでしょう?	c. 行って
4.	１８日(月)のテストには______いいですか。	d. 行かなくて
5.	６日もここに______いましたよ。来月も来るんじゃないですか?	e. 来た
6.	エリザベスさんはきのうは______のですが、あさっては来るでしょうか。	f. 来て
		g. 来ません
7.	ワンさんはあのパーティーには______のでしょうか。	h. 来なかった
8.	ちょっとコンビニに______きてもいいですか。	

7-8-2R Guessing what question is being answered

For each of the following statements, suggest what question is being answered. Try saying the question orally, then write it down.

Ex. 1. ミーティングは何日ですか。
ミーティングですか。６日ですよ。

Ex. 2. ジョンソンさんは何日にいらっしゃいますか。
ジョンソンさんですか。２６日にいらっしゃいますよ。

3. ______________________________________。
９月のカラオケパーティーですか。２０日(日)ですよ。

4. ______________________________________。
ニューヨークですか。１０日からですよ。

5. ______________________________________。
１日ですか。みんな行きますよ。

6. ______________________________________。
ジョーンズさんは来ますが、スミスさんは来ないでしょう。

7. ____。
ヴェニスですか。まだ行ってないですが、行ってみたいですね。

8. ____。
カンファレンスですか。２月じゃなくて、３月ですよ。来月です。

書き練習 Writing practice

文字練習 Symbol practice

Use the Symbol Practice sheets in Appendix A to practice kanji characters #1-4 for Scene 7-8.

7-8-3W Getting information

Each of the following is in response to a mistaken assumption you've made. Write your incorrect assumption as in the example.

Ex. 1. クラスは３日までですね？
クラスですか？３日までじゃなくて、６日までです。

Ex. 2. リサイタルは1月ですね？
リサイタルですか？１月じゃなくて、７月です。

3. ____
ミーティングですか？２日じゃなくて、２０日です。

4. ____
カンファレンスですか？３月９日じゃなくて、９月３日です。

5. ____
パーティーですか？来月じゃなくて、９月です。

6. ____
来月ですか？ジョーンズさんじゃなくて、スミスさんが行きます。

7. ____
13日ですか？スミスさんじゃなくて、ジョーンズさんが来なかったんです。

◆ Scene 7-9 練習 Practice

読み練習 Reading practice

7-9-1R Free response

Respond orally to each of the following questions that appeared in a message from a colleague. There are many possibilities. Listen to the sample audio answers.

Ex. 1. 週末（しゅうまつ）はたいてい何をしますか。
Ex. 2. ミーティングの時間は何時からなんですか。
3. このクラスのテストは何日にあるんですか。
4. あのイベントは 4 時半から何時までですか。
5. あのインターンは 1 日ですか、半日ですか。
6. 何月にハワイに行くんですか。
7. あのアルバイトはここには何日いますか。
8. あのアルバイトはここには何日に来ますか。

7-9-2R Which time word is missing?

For each question, identify from the selection below which time word is missing.

a. 時間	b. この間	c. 何時	d. 1時半	e. きょう	f. 1時間

Ex. 1. バスで行きたいんですけど、___a___ありますか。
Ex. 2. ___b___はどうもありがとうございました。
3. レクチャーは______からですか？
4. クラスは______にありますね？
5. ______何かすることはありますか。
6. カンファレンスはあと______ぐらいですか。

書き練習 Writing practice

文字練習 Symbol practice

Use the Symbol Practice sheets in Appendix A to practice kanji characters #5-8 for Scenes 7–9.

7-9-3W Getting information

Identify from the selection below the equivalent for each of the time descriptions you hear, and write it in the space provided. You may use the same word multiple times.

半時間	半日	半月

Ex. 1.	半日	Ex. 2.	半時間	3.	
4.		5.		6.	

◆ 評価 Assessment

Answer sheet templates are provided in Appendix B for the Assessment sections.

聞いてみよう Listening comprehension

Read the context, listen to the audio, and then answer the questions based on what you hear. If you hear something unfamiliar, focus on what you know to determine the correct answer.

1. Yoko and her friend Kawamura-san have just finished lunch at a new restaurant.
   a. What does Yoko say about the desserts at this place?
   b. What is Kawamura-san's concern about having dessert?
   c. According to Kawamura-san, what did Yoko's fiancé say? When did he say this?
   d. What does Yoko ultimately decide to do? What does she tell Kawamura-san to do?
2. It's after 7 p.m. and a few people are still working in the office. Sasha talks to a relatively new part-time worker, who is also staying in the office.
   a. What does Sasha suppose that the part-timer thinks of the work?
   b. How does the part-timer respond? What additional benefit of working there does the part-timer mention?
   c. What does Sasha apologize for?
3. Brian and his friends from the aikido club are walking up the trail on Mt. Fuji.
   a. What does Brian suggest?
   b. What reason does Brian's friend initially give for agreeing with the suggestion?
   c. What reason does Brian give for it being difficult?
   d. What reason does Brian's friend add?
   e. What question does Brian ask his friend?
   f. What is her response?
4. Brian and his friends are nearing the top of Mt. Fuji.
   a. What is the weather? How severe is the weather situation?
   b. What did Brian's friend hear about the weather? What did she not hear?
   c. Why does Brian's friend think the weather isn't unusual?
5. Eri and her friend from graduate school went to see a movie together.
   a. What did Eri think of the movie?
   b. What did her friend think of the movie?
6. Eri and her friend are talking over some coffee after going to the movie.
   a. What did Eri's friend hear?
   b. Where did the information come from? Be specific.

c. What reasons are given for why this information might not be trustworthy?
d. Which of these reasons does Eri find surprising?

7. Brian and his friend are discussing where to have lunch.

   a. What location is being discussed? What good things does Brian's friend mention about this place?
   b. Why is Brian reluctant about this location?
   c. Which location do they ultimately go with? Why do they decide on this location?
   d. Why does Brian's friend suggest *udon*?

使ってみよう Dry run

For each of the following, listen to the audio and respond to what was said based on the context.

1. When asked by a co-worker about Ikeda-san, respond with a conjecture that he (a) will do it; (b) will walk here; (c) doesn't understand English; (d) will be a little late; (e) won't write (it) by tomorrow; (f) will talk to Yamaguchi-san; (g) would say that it's not okay.
2. When asked by a co-worker about Takahashi-san, respond that you think (a) he went with his wife; (b) he said it was more spacious than here; (c) it wasn't his older brother; (d) going was by taxi, but returning was by bus.
3. When a friend makes a comment, respond (a) isn't it a little expensive?; (b) isn't she going to be late?; (c) isn't that a bit severe?; (d) isn't that not Murakami-san?
4. When a friend asks about Ikeda-kun, respond that you heard (a) he's not coming; (b) he isn't used to it yet; (c) he did it already; (d) he wasn't able to do it; (e) he was surprised; (f) it will be a problem (lit. he will be troubled).
5. Respond to a co-worker's question based on the following information: Nakamura-san is sick today.
6. You have been looking for a new apartment. Respond to a colleague's question based on the following information: You looked at an apartment. You think the size is the same, but it's cheaper than your current apartment. Additionally, it's close to the train station, so it's a nice place.
7. When a *senpai* asks who is presenting tomorrow, respond that Sasaki-san, Yamashita-san, and then Mori-san will present.
8. When a friend asks for directions to your apartment, respond that you go straight along this street, turn left at something-or-other pharmacy, and it's right there.

Now it's your turn to start the conversation based on the given context. Listen to how the other person reacts to you. For some items, you may not get a verbal response. Don't be concerned if you hear things you have not yet learned.

9. For each of the following, you are asking a question based on something you observed. Ask a friend (a) if his older sister won't be coming; (b) if he is going home already; (c) if he isn't going to talk to the teacher; (d) if he's not bringing the cake he made.

10. Your senpai is explaining that you will be taking a certain train to a meeting in Nagoya. Ask if you will be returning by the same train.
11. You're having a hard time dealing with the heat in Kyoto. Make a comment to a co-worker (lit. that one doesn't get used to the heat in Kyoto).
12. You are on your way to attend a presentation. Ask your *senpai* who the person that will be speaking is.
13. You are speaking to a representative from Aoi Shuppan. The other day Nakajima, your *koohai*, was supposed to attend a joint meeting with your company and Aoi Shuppan, but came down sick and was unable to attend. Apologize to the representative from Aoi Shuppan.
14. Assuming that the junior student knows what you are talking about, invite him to (a) write it; (b) make a request; (c) do it; (d) end it; (e) take a break; (f) go there; (g) read it.

読んでみよう Contextualized reading

Consider the context provided and read the passage to answer the questions.

(1) Here is a list of international students from the United States at Fukuzawa University.

氏名	州	出身地
ジェフリー・ジョンソン	デラウェア	ウィルミントン
ウェンディー・マーティン	カリフォルニア	サンディエゴ
ジェニファー・ウィリアムズ	ウィスコンシン	マディソン
アンドリュー・ジョーンズ	カリフォルニア	サンノゼ

a. How many female students are on the list?
b. Where is Mr. Johnson's hometown?
c. Who are from the same state? Where in that state are they from, respectively?
d. Who is from the state of Wisconsin? Where is his/her hometown?

(2) Here are some text messages between Brian and Ichiro:

DOKOKA
19:14
ブライアン・ワン
これからマーティンさんとカラオケに行くんだけど、よかったら来ない？
行きたい！何時まで？
１０時半ごろまでかなあ。

a. What invitation is made? Provide details.
b. What are they going to do? For how long?

(3) A text message Brian sent to his *senpai*, Hiromi, who occasionally visits his aikido club.

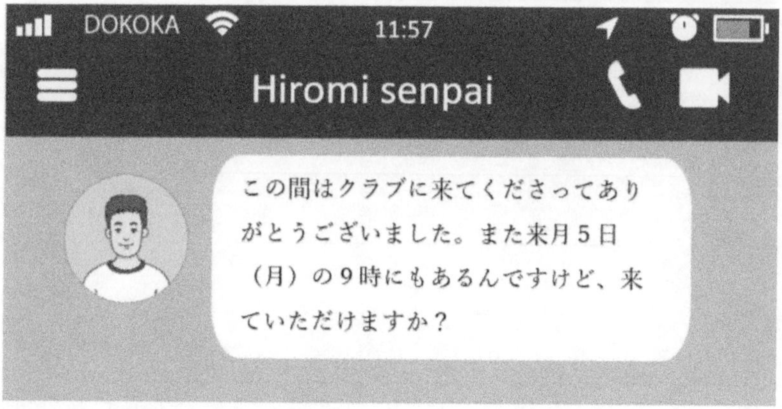
DOKOKA
11:57
Hiromi senpai
この間はクラブに来てくださってありがとうございました。また来月５日（月）の９時にもあるんですけど、来ていただけますか？

a. What is Brian thanking Hiromi for?
b. What request does Brian make? Be specific.

(4) You found the following in front of a popular family restaurant.

<u>ウェイティングリスト</u>

受付番号	お名前	受付時間	人数
1	ヤマダ	7:16	4
2	ハートフォード	7:18	6
3	~~カンダ~~	~~7:26~~	~~2~~
4	~~ヨシモト~~	~~7:28~~	~~2~~
5	シェーファー	7時半	1
6	ジョンソン	7:42	3
7			

a. What is it?
b. Who came first?
c. Which name is associated with the most number of people?
d. Who came alone? At what time?
e. Which names have been crossed out?

書き取り Dictation

Listen, imagine the context, repeat silently what you hear, then write it down.

1. ____。

2. ____。

3. ____。

4. ____。

5. ____。

6. ____。

7. ____。

8. ____。

書いてみよう Contextualized writing

Consider the context provided and compose a text according to the directions.

1. You are giving a homemade cookie to your colleague Jessica in return for the lunch she shared with you a while ago. On a sticky note attached to the container, write a thank-you note about the lunch.

2. You found a typo in the schedule that your senior colleague Mr. Ford printed. On a sticky note attached to the schedule, tell your colleague that the meeting on the day after tomorrow is from 3:30, not 3:00.

3. You are planning to go to karaoke with other friends on the 10th (M) from 19:00 to 21:30. On a sticky note, invite your friend Vivian to come, if it's alright.

知ってる? What do you know?

Select the most appropriate option and write the letter in the space on your answer sheet.

1. All –RU verbs end in __________. (BTS 1)

   a. ある and いる
   b. いる and うる
   c. いる and える

2. Which of the following is a –RU verb? (BTS 1)

   a. 帰(かえ)る
   b. 考(かんが)える
   c. 走(はし)る

3. Which of the following is a special polite ARU verb? (BTS 1)

   a. ある
   b. おっしゃる
   c. わかる

4. The consonant 'w' will show up in some forms of which verb? (BTS 1)

   a. 買(か)う
   b. いらっしゃる
   c. する

5. When you add さ to an adjective it indicates __________. (BTS 2)

   a. extent
   b. comparison
   c. type

6. You're surprised that your classmate was chosen to enter the speech contest. You ask: 上手(じょうず)_______? (BTS 4)

   a. の
   b. のだ
   c. なの

7. You're surprised to see your roommate wearing a swimsuit. You ask: 泳(およ)ぐ__________? (BTS 4)

   a. なの
   b. の
   c. のだ

8. You want to know why the new intern is waiting for the division manager. You ask:
部長と相談する______________か。(BTS 4)

a. んです
b. んだ
c. の

9. You've been asked who studied Japanese with you. You give the complete list of your fellow language learners.
スミスさんとケリーさん、__________ミラーさんも勉強しました。(BTS 5, 16)

a. それに
b. ほかに
c. それから

10. You ask your friend if her father also swims.
__________も泳ぐの？(BTS 6)

a. お父さん
b. パパ
c. 父

11. To make the ない form of U-verbs, we drop the –U from the citation form and add _____. (BTS 7)

a. *nai*
b. *anai*

12. To make the ない form of RU-verbs, we drop the –RU from the citation form and add _____. (BTS 7)

a. *nai*
b. *anai*

13. Past informal affirmative verb forms that end in った are formed from citation forms that end in ________. (BTS 8)

a. す and う
b. む and る
c. る and つ

14. Which of the following verb forms have alternate forms? (BTS 8)

a. formal affirmative
b. informal negative
c. formal negative

15. You've been asked your opinion of a hotel room. You respond:
とっても静か________と思う。(BTS 12)

a. です
b. だ
c. でした

16. You think that Kimura-san made the cake, but . . . (you're not sure).
木村さんが____________________けど……。(BTS 12)

a. 作ると思った
b. 作ったと思う
c. 作ったと思って

17. You ask about the location of the economics department.
____________キャンパスですか。(BTS 15)

a. 同じ
b. 不便
c. 別

18. You ask your colleague which computer she uses a lot.
よく__________コンピューターはどれですか。(BTS 14)

a. 使った
b. 使うの
c. 使う

19. You've been asked why you like a certain café. You respond:
コーヒーが美味しいんですよ。________とっても安いんです。(BTS 16)

a. それから
b. それに
c. あと

20. You tell your host how you got to his house.
すごくきれいな道________歩いてきました。(BTS 17)

a. を
b. が
c. に

21. You can use 何とか when you__________. (BTS 19)

a. are not sure of what something is called
b. doubt what you just heard
c. remember how to pronounce a word

22. When a borrowed word contains a sound not found in Japanese, __________. (BTL 1)

a. it is represented in romaji
b. katakana can be adapted to represent it
c. another word is substituted

23. The ん of んです _______. (BTL 2)

a. is a contracted form of の
b. never appears in written Japanese
c. may be な or の, depending on context

24. English morae that begin with an /f/ in English are represented by _______ in expanded spelling. (BTL 3)

a. フ + ア, イ, エ, or オ
b. フ + small ァ, ィ, ェ, or ォ
c. ホ + small ァ, ィ, ェ, or ォ

25. Syllables beginning with a /w/ sound (other than those represented by ワ or ウ) are represented by _______ in expanded spelling. (BTL 4)

a. ウ + イ, エ, or オ
b. ワ + small ィ, ェ, or ォ
c. ウ + small ィ, ェ, or ォ

26. Syllables beginning with /sh/ and /j/ before "long a" and "short e" are represented by _______ in expanded spelling. (BTL 5)

a. シェ and ジェ
b. シェ and ジェ
c. テェ and デェ

27. Words with /t/ or /d/ before "long e" or "short i" are represented by _______ in expanded spelling. (BTL 6)

a. トィ and ドィ
b. チィ and ヂィ
c. ティ and ディ

28. /v/ morae may be represented by _______ in expanded spelling. (BTL 7)

a. ウ + small ァ, ィ, ェ, or ォ
b. ワ + small ァ, ィ, ェ, or ォ
c. ヴ + small ァ, ィ, ェ, or ォ

29. Words with /kw/ (as in *quick*) will be represented by _______ in expanded spelling. (BTL 8)

a. カ+ small ァ, ィ, ェ, or ォ
b. コ+ small ァ, ィ, ェ, or ォ
c. ク+ small ァ, ィ, ェ, or ォ

30. Words with /ts/ before /a/, /i/, /e/, or/o/ (as in Mozart) will be represented by ________ in expanded spelling. (BTL 9)

   a. チ+ small ァ, ィ, ェ, or ォ
   b. ツ+ small ァ, ィ, ェ, or ォ
   c. テ+ small ァ, ィ, ェ, or ォ

31. The Japanese pronunciation of a kanji is called ________. (BTL 10)

   a. onyomi
   b. kunyomi
   c. kana

32. The stroke order for kanji is important because ________. (BTL 11)

   a. if you do not use correct stroke order, the cursive version is impossible to write
   b. if you use a stylus to write characters in an online app, the app will not recognize a character if the strokes are in the wrong order
   c. both a and b

33. Okurigana refers to hiragana that is used to ________. (BTL 12)

   a. write the endings for Verbs and Adjectives
   b. represent words that are not written in kanji
   c. tell how a kanji is pronounced

34. How many kanji are taught in grades 1 through 12 in Japan? (BTL 13)

   a. 2136
   b. 5869
   c. 7510

35. Radicals are________. (BTL 15)

   a. kanji combinations necessary for reading
   b. repeating parts of kanji
   c. the kanji taught in elementary school

第 8 幕
Act 8

おめでとうございます。

Congratulations.

◆ Scene 8-1 練習 Practice

理解練習 Comprehension practice

8-1-1C What's happening?

What important event is discussed in each conversation? Select from the pool of options provided.

Ex. 1. __h__ Ex. 2. __e__ 3. ______ 4. ______
5. ______ 6. ______ 7. ______ 8. ______

a. Birthday	b. Marriage	c. Divorce	d. Graduation
e. Promotion	f. New job	g. Study abroad	h. College entrance

8-1-2C I do it every. . . (BTS 3)

Listen to each conversation, and select from the pool of descriptions the time word that is mentioned.

Ex. 1. __i__ Ex. 2. __b__ 3. ______ 4. ______
5. ______ 6. ______ 7. ______ 8. ______

a. Every day	b. Every year	c. Every month	d. Every morning
e. Every semester	f. Every hour	g. Every time	h. Every evening
i. Every week			

実演練習 Performance practice

8-1-3P Urging someone to try doing something (BTS 1)

When Kimura-san, a new member of your group, shows some interest in an activity, urge her to try it.

Ex. 1.

Kimura-san	あれを登るんですね？面白そうですね。	So you climb that, right? Looks interesting!
You	面白いですよ。木村さんも登ってみませんか？	It is interesting. Kimura-san, won't you try climbing it, too?

Ex. 2.

Kimura-san	毎日走るんですね？いいですねえ。	So you run every day, right? It must be good!
You	いいですよ。木村さんも走ってみませんか？	It is good. Kimura-san, won't you try running, too?

3.	4.	5.

6.	**7.**	**8.**

8-1-4P Asking what kind (BTS 2)

When Ikeda-san, a new member of your group, shows an interest in something, inquire what kind he likes.

Ex. 1.

Ikeda-san	よく食べますよ、ケーキ。わりと好きなんですよ。	I eat them often, cakes. It's that I rather like them.
You	へえ、どんなケーキが好きですか？	Is that right? What kind of cake do you like?

Ex. 2.

Ikeda-san	映画はね、ほとんど毎週見ますねえ。	Movies? I see one almost every week.
You	へえ。どんな映画が好きですか？	Is that right? What kind of movies do you like?

8-1 腕試し Tryout

1. Congratulate someone on a special event, such as a birthday, graduation, marriage, or getting a job.
2. Give someone a present on an occasion such as a birthday, graduation, marriage, etc.
3. Invite someone to do an activity that they have never done before.

◆ Scene 8-2 練習 Practice

理解練習 Comprehension practice

8-2-1C Affirmative and negative requests (BTS 4)

Listen to the conversation, then select the verb that appears in the request from the pool of options, and mark whether the request is affirmative or negative.

Ex. 1.	i	☐ Affirmative	☒ Negative
Ex. 2.	h	☒ Affirmative	☐ Negative
3.	______	☐ Affirmative	☐ Negative
4.	______	☐ Affirmative	☐ Negative
5.	______	☐ Affirmative	☐ Negative
6.	______	☐ Affirmative	☐ Negative
7.	______	☐ Affirmative	☐ Negative
8.	______	☐ Affirmative	☐ Negative
9.	______	☐ Affirmative	☐ Negative

a. Ride	b. See	c. Open	d. Wait	e. Say	f. Know
g. Show	h. Decide	i. Use	j. Laugh	k. Come	l. Buy

8-2-2C Giving reasons (BTS 5)

In each of the following, listen to what Hashimoto-san (the woman) says and select the option that best reflects the nuance of what Hashimoto-san is saying: (a) as an explanation of her circumstance; (b) as an explicit reason for something; (c) as a circumstance that she feels should be obvious to the other person.

Ex. 1. c	Ex. 2. a	3. ______	4. ______	5. ______	6. ______
7. ______	8. ______	9. ______	10. ______	11. ______	

実演練習 Performance practice

8-2-3P Requesting to stop (BTS 4)

Gently but firmly ask Takeda-san, who is junior to you, to not do something.

Ex. 1.		
Takeda-san	会議の話題、変えてもいいですか？	Is it all right if I changed the topic of the conference?
You	いえ、やっぱり変えないでくださいませんか？	No, I've thought about it—would you mind not changing it?
Ex. 2.		
Takeda-san	忘れ物、もういらないんじゃないですか？捨てますよ。	We don't need (to keep) these lost and found items. I'll throw them away, okay?
You	いえ、やっぱり捨てないでくださいませんか？	No, I've thought about it—would you mind not throwing them away?

8-2 腕試し Tryout

In a casual conversation with someone, try to add a little humor to the conversation, and pay attention to how the other person responds. Be careful!

◆ Scene 8-3 練習 Practice

理解練習 Comprehension practice

8-3-1C Invitation to do what? (BTS 7, 8)

In each of the following, you are invited to do something by a family member of your friend while staying over at their home. Write down what you are invited to do, using the suggestions in the box below as a reference.

Ex. 1. Enter the house ______ Ex. 2. Relax ______

3. ______ 4. ______

5. ______ 6. ______

7. ______ 8. ______

9. ______ 10. ______

11. ______ 12. ______

Enter the house	Come again	Relax	Sleep	Be comfortable
Rest a bit	Sit	Don't hold back	Drink tea	Have breakfast
Use an extra blanket	Use an umbrella	Take care	Use a towel	

実演練習 Performance practice

8-3-2P Approving ideas for action (BTS 8)

You are working on a presentation with Ōno-san, who has a lot of great ideas. Respond to all of his requests by urging him to do the thing he asks to do.

Ex. 1.

Ōno-san	じゃあ、プレゼンの時間、こちらで決めてもいいですか?	So, is it all right if our side decides on the time of the presentation?
You	あ、いいですよ。どうぞお決めください。	Sure. Please decide.

Ex. 2.

Ōno-san	このこと、うちの部長ともう一度相談してもいいですか?	Is it all right if I consulted about this with my division chief one more time?
You	あ、いいですよ。どうぞご相談ください。	Sure. Please consult (with her).

8-3 腕試し Tryout

1. When visiting a Japanese household, be a considerate guest by presenting a gift, showing appreciation, holding back as appropriate, and engaging in comfortable social talk with your hosts.
2. When you have invited your friends—people to whom you do not need to use polite language—to your home, urge them to engage in various activities (e.g., come in, relax, don't hold back, eat, drink, etc.).

◆ Scene 8-4 練習 Practice

理解練習 Comprehension practice

8-4-1C How often? (BTS 10)

Listen to various people responding to questions about their experience eating sushi in Japan. What are they saying about their experience? Select from the options provided below.

Ex. 1. __e__	Ex. 2. __d__	3. ______	4. ______
5. ______	6. ______		

a. I always do it.
b. I have not done it a few times (i.e., I almost always do).
c. I occasionally don't (i.e., but I do more often than not).
d. There are times when I do.
e. I have (i.e., at least once, maybe not more than that).
f. I never have.

実演練習 Performance practice

8-4-2P Showing reluctance (BTS 10)

Your friend is eager to have you try something. Show your reluctance by telling her that you have done it in the past.

Ex. 1.

Friend	一度この公園を走ってみません?気持ちいいですよ!	Do you want to try running around this park once? It feels great!
You	でも、走ったことありますけど……。	But, I've already run (around the park) before, so. . .

Ex. 2.

Friend	一度こっちを使ってみません?使いやすいですよ!	Do you want to try using this once? It's easy to use!
You	でも、使ったことありますけど……。	But, I've already used it before, so. . .

8-4-3P Telling someone that you haven't done something before (BTS 10)

Saito-san, a work colleague, is curious whether or not you've ever done something before. Respond that you haven't yet, but would like to.

Ex. 1.

Saito-san	新幹線を使ったことありますか。	Have you ever used the bullet train?
You	まだ使ったことないんですけど、一度使ってみたいですね。	I haven't yet, but I'd like to try it once.

Ex. 2.

Saito-san	ヨーロッパに行ったことありますか。	Have you ever been to Europe?
You	まだ行ったことないんですけど、一度行ってみたいですね。	I haven't yet, but I'd like to try going there once.

8-4-4P Sometimes I don't do it. (BTS 10)

Fujita-san, a friend, is under the impression that you do (or don't do) something, but the situation isn't as extreme as he's thinking. Tell him that there are times when you don't do (or do) the thing.

Ex. 1.

Saito-san	いつもタウンシネマに行くでしょう?	You always go to Town Cinema, right?
You	まあ、行かないこともあるけどね。	Well, there are times when I don't go, you know.

Ex. 2.

Saito-san	うどんは全然食べないでしょう?	You don't eat udon, right?
You	まあ、食べることもあるけどね。	Well, there are times when I do eat it, you know.

8-4 腕試し Tryout

1. When the opportunity presents itself, visit someone's home. Before going, select a gift that you feel will balance the burden of your visit without overdoing it. When you visit, appropriately give the gift as a token of appreciation for being invited.
2. Ask some acquaintances about their prior experiences. For example, you could ask if they've ever been to your home country.

◆ Scene 8-5 練習 Practice

理解練習 Comprehension practice

8-5-1C Being an engaged listener (BTS 14)

In audio 1, you will hear a conversation in which one speaker tells a story (something that happened that was embarrassing, scary, etc.). The other person, after prompting the story, will be mainly listening, using various 相槌 as he listens. Shadow the listening person; that is, whenever he uses verbal 相槌, say it along with him. Listen again and see if you can predict the placement and type of 相槌, even if you don't understand everything you are hearing. Remember, the other person may also be nodding or changing his facial expressions without necessarily making any sound.

In audio 2, you will hear only one side of the conversation. This time play the part of an engaged listener by using the 相槌 you practiced when shadowing the listener in audio 1.

8-5-2C What's about to happen? (BTS 12)

Your senior colleague makes predictions about the immediate future. What does he say is about to happen? The selection of answers is provided in the box.

Ex. 1.	Laugh	Ex. 2.	Forget
3.		4.	
5.		6.	
7.		8.	
9.		10.	

Laugh	Cry	Forget	Become thirsty	Become hungry
Become lost	Clear up	Wake up	Begin	Be able to talk

実演練習 Performance practice

8-5-3P Agreeing with an observation (BTS 12)

Your senior colleague, Ikeda-san, wonders out loud about another colleague. Agree with his thinking by making an observation of your own.

Ex. 1.

Ikeda-san	嬉しいのかなあ、山田君。	I wonder if Yamada-kun is happy.
You	確かに嬉しそうに見えますね。	He certainly seems happy, doesn't he.

Ex. 2.

Ikeda-san	仕事、きついのかな、山田君。	I wonder if the job is hard for Yamada-kun.
You	確かにきつそうに見えますね。	It certainly seems hard, doesn't it.

8-5-4P I think he probably will. (BTS 13)

When Maeda-san, your *senpai*, asks about what Sato-kun will do, respond that you think Sato-kun will probably do it.

Ex. 1.

Maeda-san	忙しそうだね、佐藤君。今日は来ないかなあ。	Sato-kun seems busy. I wonder if he won't come today.
You	来るだろうと思いますけど……。	I think he'll probably come, but. . .

Ex. 2.

Maeda-san	あの仕事はちょっときつそうだね。佐藤君はできるかな。	This job seems a bit rough. I wonder if Sato-kun can do it.
You	できるだろうと思いますけど……。	I think he can probably do it, but. . .

8-5 腕試し Tryout

1. Listen to someone tell you a story in Japanese, and use 相槌(あいづち) to show that you are listening.
2. Describe the personality (i.e., the kind of person they are) of someone you know to someone else.

◆ Scene 8-6 練習 Practice

理解練習 Comprehension practice

8-6-1C How often does this happen? (BTS 15)

Listen to the conversations, and for each activity write how frequently the activity is done.

Ex. 1.	Wanting to go to New York:	Sometimes
Ex. 2.	Practicing golf:	2 or 3 times a week
3.	Going to English class:	______________
4.	Going to Hokkaido:	______________
5.	Going to concerts:	______________
6.	Making curry at home:	______________
7.	Going to a *shogi* class:	______________

8-6-2C How many? (BTS 17)

Listen to each statement, and write the quantity mentioned and what the quantity refers to, using the pool of options as a reference. Then mark whether it was more or less than expected.

Ex. 1.	fifty people	☒ More than expected	☐ Less than expected
Ex. 2.	one pen	☐ More than expected	☒ Less than expected
3.	______________	☐ More than expected	☐ Less than expected
4.	______________	☐ More than expected	☐ Less than expected
5.	______________	☐ More than expected	☐ Less than expected
6.	______________	☐ More than expected	☐ Less than expected
7.	______________	☐ More than expected	☐ Less than expected
8.	______________	☐ More than expected	☐ Less than expected
9.	______________	☐ More than expected	☐ Less than expected

People	Presentations	Tests	Posters	Jobs	Semesters
Classes	Pens	Times	Cakes	Hours	Cookies

実演練習 Performance practice

8-6-3P Reassuring (BTS 17)

Your friend, Yamamoto-san, shows some concern about the possibility of an extreme situation. Reassure her that the reality is very different, as far as this year is concerned.

Ex. 1.

Yamamoto-san	不便なところへの出張、何回もあるんですか?	Do you have a number of business trips to places that are inconvenient?
You	とんでもない。今年はまだ１回もありません。	Heavens no! This year, there hasn't been one.

Ex. 2.

Yamamoto-san	練習しない学生、何人もいるんですか?	Do you have a number of students who don't practice?
You	とんでもない。今年はまだ１人もいません。	Heavens no! This year, there hasn't been one.

8-6-4P Reporting surpassed expectations (BTS 13, 16, 1)

Your supervisor, Watanabe-san, asks about an event. For each number she mentions, state that you had a similar expectation, but the actual number was as much as double that. Be prepared to do some simple arithmetic!

Ex. 1.

Watanabe-san	何人ぐらい来ました?15人ぐらい?	About how many people came? 15 or so?
You	私も１５、6人だろうと思っていたんですけど、実は30人も来たんです。びっくりしました。	I'd thought probably 15 or 16, too, but actually, as many as 30 came! I was surprised.

Ex. 2.

Watanabe-san	いくらぐらいかかりました?５０万円ぐらい?	About how much did it cost? 500,000 yen or so?
You	私も５、６０万円だろうと思っていたんですけど、実は１００万円もかかったんです。びっくりしました。	I'd thought probably 500,000 or 600,000 yen, too, but actually, it cost as much as 1 million yen! I was surprised.

8-6 腕試し Tryout

1. Ask someone what they usually do when they have vacation.
2. Ask someone what the weather is like during various seasons in the place that they are from.

◆ Scene 8-7 練習 Practice

読み練習 Reading practice

8-7-1R Identifying dates and times

Say each of the dates listed in various styles and answer the questions that follow.

三月九日
2018年3月30日
六月七日（日）
一月五日（月）
八月二日（日）四時
七月九日（月）八時半
二〇〇一年九月一日
一九八六年五月二〇日

Ex. 1. What month and date is associated with the year 2001? <u>September 1st</u>

Ex. 2. List the dates specified for March. <u>9th and 30th</u>

3. Which dates are specified as Sunday? ____________

4. What day is July 9th? What is the time specified on this day? ____________

5. What year is the furthest in the past? What month and day are specified for that year? ____________

8-7-2R Answering questions about the menu

Orally answer the questions in the audio, using the information from a menu on the wall of a small eatery. Then compare your response to the audio. In addition, practice discussing what items are offered for how much and practice making orders. As needed, search online for images of some of the items.

そば 四〇〇円
うどん 四五〇円
ざるそば 五五〇円
きつねうどん 六〇〇円
たぬきうどん 六五〇円

アサヒビール 三〇〇円
キリンビール 三〇〇円
オリオンビール三五〇円

書き練習 Writing practice

文字練習 Symbol practice

Use the Symbol Practice sheets in Appendix A to practice kanji characters #9-25 for Scene 8-7.

8-7-3W Writing down prices

Listen to the voicemail and write down the prices in kanji on the menu.

ラーメン	Ex. 1. 三八〇円
しょうゆラーメン	Ex. 2. 四五〇円
みそラーメン	______
ねぎみそラーメン	______
とんこつラーメン	______
バターコーンラーメン	______

◆ Scene 8-8 練習 Practice

読み練習 Reading practice

8-8-1R Reacting with an appropriate *aizuchi*

Read the following statements and select an appropriate 相槌(あいづち) from the selection provided.

Ex. 1.	このカップル、今年で１０年目になるんだって。	(そうなんだ・そうだね)
Ex. 2.	あのインターン、今日で４日目になるけど、だめそうだね。	(やっぱり・なるほど)
3.	あの人、ビールもう３本目だって。	(へえ・よかった)
4.	２人目の人のスピーチ、おもしろそうじゃない?	(たしかに・ふうん)
5.	今月だけでもう３万人も来てるんだって。	(たしかに・ふうん)
6.	今日は６時間目のクラスがないから、５時間だけなんだよね?	(そうなんだ・そうだね)
7.	これはインドネシア語なんだって。	(なるほど・そうだね)
8.	今はまだだめだから来ないでって。	(やっぱり・たしかに)

8-8-2R Reporting a request

Read the following requests and report the content as the writer's desire to another person who may need the information. Listen to the sample reporting and response in the audio.

Ex. 1.	今日はスペイン語でお願いしたいのですが……。
Ex. 2.	今月からお願いできないでしょうか。
3.	二日間ほどお願いしたいんですけど……。
4.	三時間目のこと、お願いします。
5.	五人の人にお願いできないでしょうか?
6.	一人二万円ずつお願いしてもいいですか。
7.	六時半にお願いできますか。
8.	あの人にはお願いしないでください。

書き練習 Writing practice

文字練習 Symbol practice

Use the Symbol Practice sheets in Appendix A to practice kanji characters #26-29 for Scene 8-8.

8-8-3W What language is it?

Type in the following expressions and 何語 in a search bar on the Internet (e.g. メルシー何語) to find out what language each expression is. Then write down the language.

Ex. 1. 「メルシー」 フランス語

Ex. 2. 「オラ」 スペイン語、ポルトガル語

3. 「セウラマット シアン」 ________________

4. 「タム　ビエッ」 ________________

5. 「スパシーバ」 ________________

6. 「ダンケ」 ________________

7. 「ボンジョルノ」 ________________

◆ Scene 8-9 練習 Practice

読み練習 Reading practice

8-9-1R Greetings

Fill in the blanks found in the various greetings. You may use each option only once.

Ex. 1.	じゃ、日本語の＿＿f＿＿のみなさんにもよろしく!	a. つまらないもの
Ex. 2.	先日は＿＿b＿＿ありがとう。	b. おみやげ
3.	ちょっと先に＿＿＿＿＿きます。	c. プレゼン
4.	クリントン大学の＿＿＿＿＿はどうですか?	d. プログラム
5.	フランス語のサルマン＿＿＿＿＿にもどうぞよろしくお願いします。	e. 先生
6.	先日はわざわざ＿＿＿＿＿くださってどうもありがとうございました。	f. 学生
7.	先月の＿＿＿＿＿、とてもよかったです。	g. 来て
8.	それでは、＿＿＿＿＿。	h. 行って
9.	先生、＿＿＿＿＿ですがどうぞ。	i. お先に

8-9-2R Answering questions about Japanese class

Answer orally the following questions related to your study of Japanese. Compare your response with samples provided in the audio file. Your answers should reflect your actual situation.

1. クラスの大きさはどれぐらいですか?大きいですか?
2. 学生は何人いますか?
3. クラスメートはみんな大学生ですか?
4. クラスメートはみんな大人ですか?
5. 先生はみんな日本人ですか?
6. 日本語の先生はおもしろいですか?
7. 日本に行ったことがありますか?

8 日本の大学に行ってみたいですか?

書き練習 Writing practice

文字練習 Symbol practice

Use the Symbol Practice sheets in Appendix A to practice kanji characters #30-33 for Scene 8-9.

8-9-3W Writing a guest list

Listen to the voice mail and write down what groups of people are coming and how many people are in each group.

ゲストリスト

Ex. 1.	日本人の学生	5人
Ex. 2.	アメリカ人の学生	13人
•	________	____
•	________	____
•	________	____

◆ 評価 Assessment

Answer sheet templates are provided in Appendix B for the Assessment sections.

聞いてみよう Listening comprehension

Read the context, listen to the audio, and then answer the questions based on what you hear. If you hear something unfamiliar, focus on what you know to determine the correct answer.

1. Sasha and Kanda-san are getting ready to leave the office.
   a. What does Sasha notice?
   b. What was Kanda-san worried about? Why was he worried about this?
2. Sasha engages Kanda-san in small talk on their way to an appointment.
   a. What does Kanda-san say about 6 o'clock?
   b. What does Sasha say about 10 o'clock?
   c. What does Kanda-san say he does occasionally?
3. Sasha's fellow intern, Mizuno-san, has just returned to work after being absent for a week.
   a. Why was Mizuno-san absent?
   b. For what does Mizuno-san thank Sasha?
   c. How does Mizuno-san characterize her husband?
4. Kanda-san is talking to a college student who is a potential recruit.
   a. What does the student want to know about?
   b. What does she find out?
5. Brian and Suzuki-san are looking at a travel pamphlet about a place up north.
   a. Has either of them been there? How many times? For what?
   b. What apparently is the best season to visit the place?
6. Suzuki-san and Brian are working together on a task at their aikido dojo when Suzuki-san stops with a puzzled face.
   a. What is Suzuki-san puzzled about?
   b. How does Suzuki-san describe the thing she is puzzled about?

7. A new member at Brian's aikido dojo is talking to Brian about Kawakami-san, the head of the dojo.
    a. Where is Kawakami-san?
    b. What question can Brian not answer?
    c. Why can't Brian give the answer?
8. Suzuki-san and Brian are talking about Brian's home in the US.
    a. What new word does Brian learn from Suzuki-san? What does it mean?
    b. Where do Brian's parents live?
9. Kanda-san is visiting the office of another division.
    a. What concern does Kanda-san express?
    b. How is the concern addressed?
10. Kanda-san lends Sasha an umbrella.
    a. What does Sasha notice about the umbrella?
    b. What does she learn about it from Kanda-san?
    c. Why does Sasha apologize?
    d. What promise does she make?
11. Sasha has just finished reading a message.
    a. Who is the message from?
    b. What kind of message has apparently been received?
    c. How does Sasha describe the sender?
    d. What does Kanda-san say about the sender?
12. Sasha and Kanda-san continue to talk about the message Sasha just read.
    a. What does Sasha suggest?
    b. What does Kanda-san suggest?

使ってみよう Dry run

For each of the following, listen to the audio and respond to what was said based on the context.

1. You are speaking to an office associate. You use the item under discussion (a) once every morning; (b) fourteen to fifteen times every month; (c) twenty to thirty times every year; (d) seven to eight times every week; (e) twice every day.

2. You are speaking to a friend. Tell him (a) the test looks easy; (b) the task looks tiresome; (c) the classroom sounds noisy; (d) the division head looks serious; (e) the person next door looks kind; (f) the third floor sounds quiet; (g) the campus appears to be convenient; (h) the dining hall seems to be warm; (i) the *senpai* looks happy.
3. You are speaking to an office associate. Respond to his question or comment by offering to (a) try using it; (b) try changing them; (c) try stopping by; (d) try taking a picture and enlarging it; (e) try consulting Yagi-bucho; (f) try going back.
4. You are speaking to your office associate. When he reminds you of a task that you have never heard about, protest by indicating that you have never heard about what he just mentioned.
5. You are talking to your friend. Gently criticize her behavior by reminding her that she readily (a) changes the subject; (b) cracks awkward jokes; (c) leaves things behind; (d) forgets important names; (e) gets hungry; (f) says things that disregard filial piety; (g) becomes frightening.
6. When you are given a compliment from a *senpai*, respond that it's nothing like that.
7. When an acquaintance asks about how often you do an activity, tell her that (a) you practice almost every day; (b) you sometimes walk (there); (c) as a rule, you run at the park every Saturday morning; (d) you do it occasionally.
8. You and a friend of yours are talking about a certain book that you both really like. Respond to his comment by mentioning that you've read it three times.
9. When a *senpai* at work asks if Suzuki-san will be coming, respond that you think she probably will come.

Now it's your turn to start the conversation based on the given context. Listen to how the other person reacts to you. For some items, you may not get a verbal response. Don't be concerned if you hear things you have not yet learned.

10. Congratulate your *senpai* on his (a) graduation; (b) birthday; (c) new employment; (d) marriage.
11. Congratulate your *koohai* on her (a) graduation; (b) birthday; (c) new employment; (d) marriage.
12. You are speaking to a young *koohai*. Tell him not to (a) forget; (b) cry; (c) quit; (d) laugh; (e) sleep yet.
13. You are hosting some people at your home. Urge your guests to (a) come in; (b) sit down (in the place you point to); (c) have some tea; (d) relax; (e) not hold back; (f) come by again.
14. You are having a casual conversation with your friend. Find out if he has ever (a) climbed Mt. Fuji; (b) seen a photo of Mt. Fuji in winter; (c) thought he might want to try and visit Hokkaido; (d) been to Europe by himself; (e) seen a movie about Africa; (f) eaten Australian sweets.
15. You are speaking to your office supervisor about the workers that you oversee. Report to her that (a) Mizuno-san never comes later than 8:30 a.m.; (b) Yamashita-san never once forgets appointments; (c) there are times when Ikeda-san takes a long time on a job; (d) there are times when Yoshida-san doesn't report things properly; (e) there are times when Wada-san made decisions all by herself and didn't tell others.

読んでみよう Contextualized reading

(1) You received the following handwritten memo attached to a wrapped box.

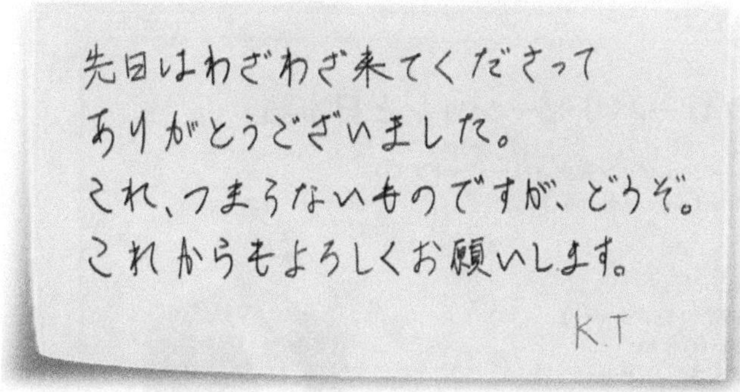
先日はわざわざ来てくださって
ありがとうございました。
これ、つまらないものですが、どうぞ。
これからもよろしくお願いします。
K.T

a. What does the writer thank you for?
b. What is likely inside the box?
c. What does the last line of the memo indicate as far as the writer's perspective on the relationship with you? (Select one.)
   (1) K.T. wants to initiate the relationship.
   (2) K.T. wishes to continue the good relationship.
   (3) K.T. wants to change the nature of the relationship.

(2) The following is a group chat history between Sasha and Eri.

a. What are they talking about?
b. How much is it? What does Sasha initially think of the price?
c. What explanation does Eri provide? How does Sasha react?

(3) The following is a flyer you received from JLC about an upcoming seminar.

「グローバリゼーションと日本語」

ゲスト：スティーブ・ジョンソン先生（ハーバード大学）
スポンサー：Japanese Language Club (JLC)

日時：２月６日（月）
- ４時半～５時半（レクチャー）
- ５時半～６時（Q&A）

場所：フレンドーホール　１８０

リフレッシュメントもあります。ぜひ来てください！

a. What is the topic of the seminar?
b. What is the name of the guest? Where is he from?
c. When is the event? What is the schedule? Where is it?
d. What will be provided for those who come to the seminar?

書き取り Dictation

Listen, imagine the context, repeat silently what you hear, then write it down.

1. ____。
2. ____。
3. ____。
4. ____。
5. ____。
6. ____。
7. ____。
8. ____。

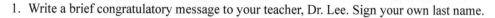

書いてみよう Contextualized writing

1. Write a brief congratulatory message to your teacher, Dr. Lee. Sign your own last name.

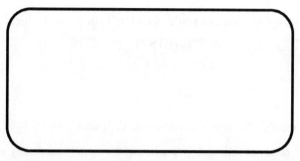

2. You brought something for your colleague in return for the souvenir she gave you. On a thank you note, thank your colleague for bringing you a souvenir the other day. Then humbly invite her to accept this. Request her continued support. Sign your last name.

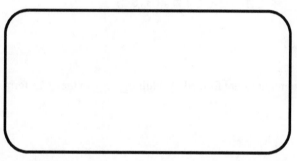

3. Using appropriate software, create a PDF file for a flyer for an upcoming seminar by typing up the following information in Japanese. Follow the format of the flyer provided in the contextualized reading #3. The kanji for *basho* 'location' is 場所.

Title: "Internship Programs in Japan"

Guest Speaker: Dr. Karen Callahan
Date/Time: 3/8(M)

- 9:30~10:30 Lecture
- 10:30~11:30 Panel Discussion

Location: Union Building Seminar Room C
There will be lunch. Please come!

知ってる? What do you know?

Select the most appropriate option and write the letter on your answer sheet.

1. You tell your companion that you'd like to try to make the recipe.
   これ作(つく)って ________ んです。(BTS 1)
   a. ほしい
   b. みたい
   c. したい
2. How does the こんな series differ from the この series? (BTS 2)
   a. noun の does not follow こんな whereas it comes immediately after この
   b. noun の can follow こんな whereas it cannot follow この
   c. この is followed by a particle whereas こんな is followed by a noun
3. You express your amazement when another student tells you how difficult the test was.
   ________ 難(むず)しかったんですか。(BTS 2)
   a. そんな
   b. そんなの
   c. そんなに
4. Negative commands are formed by adding _____ to the ない form of verbs. (BTS 4)
   a. て
   b. で
   c. よ
5. Negative commands can be made into requests by adding ________ to the command form. (BTS 4)
   a. ください
   b. よね
   c. お願(ねが)いします
6. You should be careful about using んですから to express reason because it can sound ______ . (BTS 5)
   a. doubtful
   b. childish
   c. accusatory
7. When you visit someone's home, upon entering the house you say ________. (BTS 7)
   a. お願(ねが)いします
   b. お邪魔(じゃま)します
   c. ただいま

8. When welcoming a guest to your home, you can say __________. (BTS 7)

a. よろしくお願いします

b. お世話になります

c. よくいらっしゃいました

9. In general, either the polite prefix お or ご attaches to a word depending on the word's ________________. (BTS 8)

a. usage

b. origin

c. meaning

10. You tell your coworker that sometimes you bike to the office (but you usually take the train).

自転車で ________________よ。(BTS 10)

a. 来ることもある

b. 来たことがある

c. 来ないことはない

11. You've been asked if you've ever used a certain app. You reply:

はい、一度だけ ________________。(BTS 10)

a. 使うことがある

b. 使ったことがある

c. 使わなかったことはない

12. You've been asked if you practice before every tennis lesson. You reply that you always do.

練習 ____________。(BTS 10)

a. したことがあります

b. しないことはないです

c. しなかったはあります

13. You've been asked if you've ever consulted with the teacher. You reply that you never have.

いいえ、先生と相談 ______________。(BTS 10)

a. したことはない

b. しないことはない

c. しなかったことはある

14. You're looking at a photo of a child and comment that she looks lonely.

________ 子供ですねえ。(BTS 12)

a. 寂しいの

b. 寂しそうな

c. 寂しいだろう

15. For which of the following do we find さ in the ～そう form? (BTS 12)

a. いい、ない

b. する、来(く)る

c. 大変(たいへん)、元気(げんき)

16. You've been asked if the curry rice is spicy. You think it probably is.

ええ、___________ と思(おも)う。(BTS 12, 13)

a. 辛(から)いだろう

b. 辛(から)そうだ

c. 辛(から)いこともある

17. Using 相槌(あいづち) can convey that you are _______. (BTS 14)

a. doubting what you hear
b. demanding attention
c. listening intently

18. You've been asked how often you go to the movies. You reply that you go occasionally.

__________ 行(い)きます。(BTS 15)

a. たまに

b. たいてい

c. 必(かなら)ず

19. You're irked that your friends didn't wait even one minute for you.

__________ 待(ま)たなかったんだよ。(BTS 17)

a. 1分(ぷん)

b. 1分(ぷん)も

c. もう1分(ぷん)

20. Conventions for using hiragana, katakana, and kanji are often disregarded ______. (BTL 1)

a. for the sake of clarity
b. in the case of numbers
c. for stylistic reasons

21. Kanji are used for writing numbers ________. (BTL 2)

a. in vertical writing
b. on price tags
c. when the writer wants to be clear

22. Which of the following are frequently assigned kanji on the basis of pronunciation? (BTL 3)

a. days of the week
b. food items
c. place names

第 9 幕
Act 9

一番(いちばん)好(す)きなのは……。

My favorite one is . . .

好(す)きこそものの上手(じょうず)なれ

What one likes, one does well.

◆ Scene 9-1 練習 Practice

理解練習 Comprehension practice

9-1-1C Identifying Sentence Modifiers (BTS 1)

In each conversation you will hear a Sentence Modifier. Write the noun that is modified under "Noun," and the description provided by the Sentence Modifier under "Modifier."

	Noun	Modifier
Ex. 1.	Person	Always studies English at the big table on the 6th floor of the library
Ex. 2.	Physics textbook	Ikeda-kun borrowed last month
3.		
4.		
5.		
6.		
7.		

9-1-2C Confirming something (BTS 2)

Murata-san is confirming something with an office associate. Listen to the audio and select the context that best matches her question.

Section A. Murata-san is confirming

Ex. 1. ___a___ Ex. 2. ___d___ 3. ________ 4. ________

a. who said it: that it was Ikegami-san that said New York was scary.
b. what was scary: that it was New York that Ikegami-san said was scary.
c. what was said: that "New York is scary" was the thing that Ikegami-san said.
d. what happened: that Ikegami-san said that New York was scary.

Section B. Murata-san is confirming

5. ______________ 6. ______________ 7. ______________ 8. ______________

a. who did it: that it was Hiroshi that asked Sakamoto-sensei about the homework yesterday.
b. what it was: that the thing that Hiroshi asked Sakamoto-sensei about yesterday was the homework.
c. when it was: that it was yesterday that Hiroshi asked Sakamoto-sensei about the homework.
d. what happened: that Hiroshi asked Sakamoto-sensei about the homework yesterday.

Section C. Murata-san is confirming

9. ______________ 10. ______________ 11. ______________ 12. ______________

a. who said it: that it was Nakatani-san that said it wouldn't be easy to come to the meeting next week.
b. what it is that's difficult: that it was next week's meeting that Nakatani-san said it wouldn't be easy to come to.
c. what was said: that "coming to next week's meeting won't be easy" is what Nakatani-san said.
d. what happened: that Nakatani-san said that it wouldn't be easy to come to next week's meeting.

実演練習 Performance practice

9-1-3P Giving permission to a particular group of people (BTS 1)

You are a supervising member of a group. When Matsumoto-san, a group member, brings something to your attention regarding him and another group member, acknowledge that you heard and then ask if there is anyone in the group in a similar situation.

Ex. 1.

Matsumoto-san	あのう、僕も山崎君も、留学生と話したいんですが……。	Um, both Yamazaki-kun and I would like to talk to the study abroad students, but . . . .
You	そうですか。留学生と話したい人、ほかにいますか？	I see. Are there others who would like to talk to the study abroad students?

Ex. 2.

Matsumoto-san	僕も池田君も、土曜日のマラソンに出るんですが……。	Uhm, both Ikeda-kun and I are participating in the marathon this Saturday, but . . .
You	そうですか。土曜日のマラソンに出る人、ほかにいますか。	I see. Are there others who are participating in the marathon this Saturday?

9-1-4P It's been done! (BTS 3)

Reassure Yagi-san, your supervisor, that the matter that she is concerned about has been taken care of.

Ex. 1.

Yagi-san	２階も、きれいに整理しましょう。	Let's tidy things up on the second floor, too.
You	あ、もうちゃんと整理してありますから。	Oh, it's all been tidied up already, so (don't worry).

Ex. 2.

Yagi-san	なるべく早くお客様にお話ししましょう。	Let's talk to the customer at our earliest opportunity.
You	あ、もうちゃんとお話ししてありますから。	Oh, (the customer) has been talked to already, so (don't worry).

◆ Scene 9-2 練習 Practice

理解練習 Comprehension practice

9-2-1C What's the amount? (BTS 6)

Write the fraction or decimal that you hear under "amount." Write what the amount refers to under "topic."

	Amount	Topic
Ex. 1.	3.75	Length
Ex. 2.	2/3	Copies
3.		
4.		
5.		
6.		
7.		

9-2-2C For what purpose? (BTS 5)

What purposes are identified by the speakers? Select from the options given.

Ex. 1. ___a___ Ex. 2. ___c___ 3. ______ 4. ______ 5. ______
6. ______ 7. ______

a. to apologize	b. to swim	c. to run
d. to retrieve something	e. to buy lunch	f. to play

実演練習 Performance practice

9-2-3P Reporting the proportions (BTS 2, 6)

Tell your supervisor what proportion of the population satisfies the condition she suggests, using information in the graphics provided.

Ex. 1.

Yagi-san	みんな全部書き終わりましたか？	Did everyone finish writing everything?
You	ええっと、全部書き終わったのは３分の１ぐらいですねえ。	Umm, those who finished writing everything are about one third of them.

Ex. 2.

Yagi-san	試験の問題、どの学生もできましたか？	Was every student able to answer the exam questions?
You	ええっと、できたのは５分の２ぐらいですねえ。	Umm, those who could are about two-fifths of them.

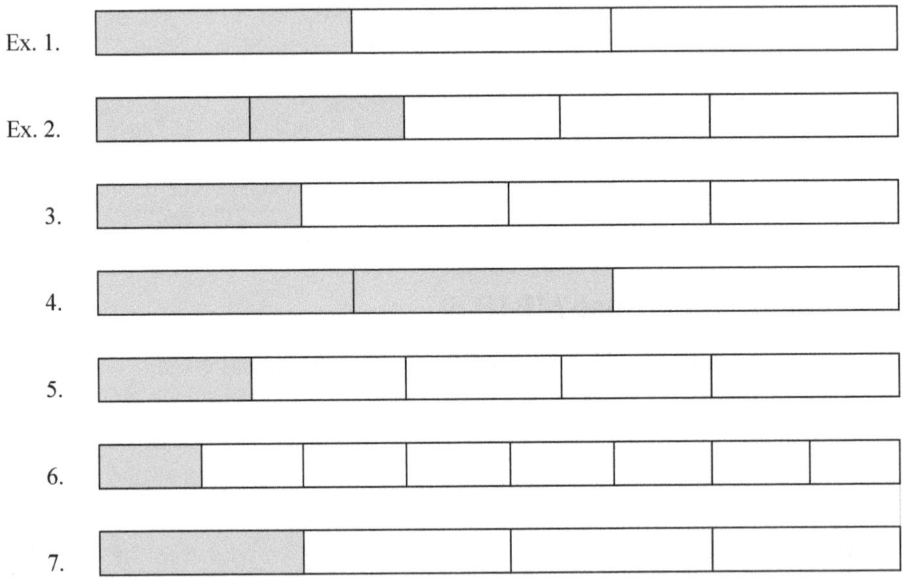

9-2-4P Let's do it (BTS 5)

When your *senpai*, Ikeda-san, says that he'd like to do something, suggest that you both go do it.

Ex. 1.

Ikeda-san	今日は泳ぎたいんだけど。	I'd like to swim a little, but . . .
You	そうですか。じゃ、泳ぎに行きましょう。	Really? Well, let's go swimming.

Ex. 2.

Ikeda-san	ちょっと新しいのを借りたいんだけど。	I'd kind of like to borrow a new one, but . . . .
You	そうですか。じゃ、借りに行きましょう。	Really? Well, let's go borrow a new one.

◆ Scene 9-3 練習 Practice

理解練習 Comprehension practice

9-3-1C What job? (BTS 7)

Write down the person's occupation in English.

Ex. 1.	IT job	Ex. 2.	Something travel related
3.	______	4.	______
5.	______	6.	______
7.	______	8.	______

実演練習 Performance practice

9-3-2P Discussing career aspirations (BTS 7, 8)

Hayashi-san, a college student you met recently, shares her career aspirations with you. Ask her why she is interested in the career option she mentions.

Ex. 1.

Hayashi-san	会社員より、公務員の方になりたいかなと思って……。	I'm thinking that I want to become a public servant rather than a regular office worker . . . .
You	ふうん。林さんはどうして公務員になりたいと思うんですか？	Hmmm, why do you think you want to be a public servant, Ms. Hayashi?

Ex. 2.

Hayashi-san	法律関係の仕事がしたくて、頑張ってます。	I'd like to do a law-related job, and I'm working hard.
You	ふうん。林さんはどうして法律関係の仕事がしたいと思うんですか？	Hmmm, why do you think you want to do a law-related job, Ms. Hayashi?

9-3-3P Giving potential reasons (BTS 8, 9)

You and your colleague, Ito-san, are discussing various people you both know. When Ito-san wonders why the person made a particular choice, suggest to him as a potential reason that a family member is in the same situation or has done the same thing. The person's influential family member is indicated in the illustration.

Ex. 1.

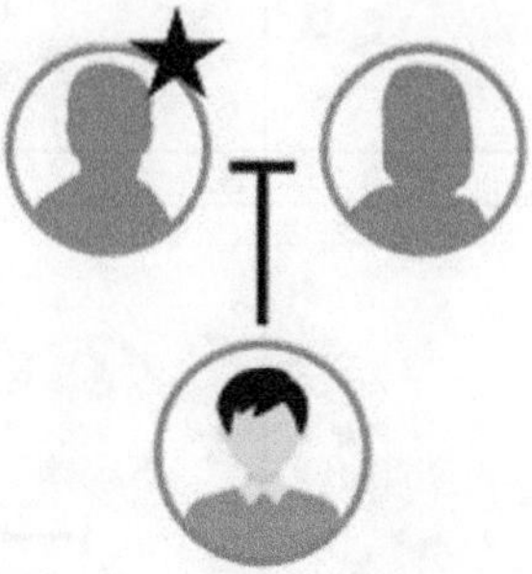

Ito-san	清水さんって九州の大学行くんですよね。どうしてかなあ。	Shimizu-san is going to a university in Kyushu, right? I wonder why.
You	まあ、お父さんも九州の大学に行ってるしね。	Well, his father has gone to a university in Kyushu too, so . . . .

Ex. 2.

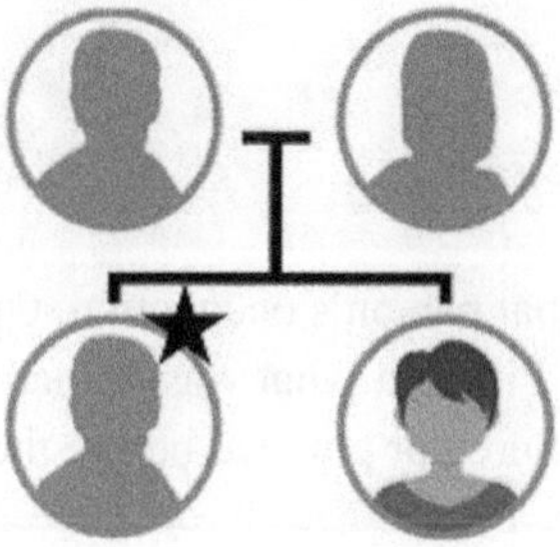

Ito-san	小林さんは法律事務所に就職するんですよね。なぜですかねえ。	Kobayashi-san is going to be employed at a law firm, right? I wonder why.
You	まあ、お兄さんも法律事務所に就職してるしね。	Well, her brother has gotten employed at a law firm, too, so . . . .

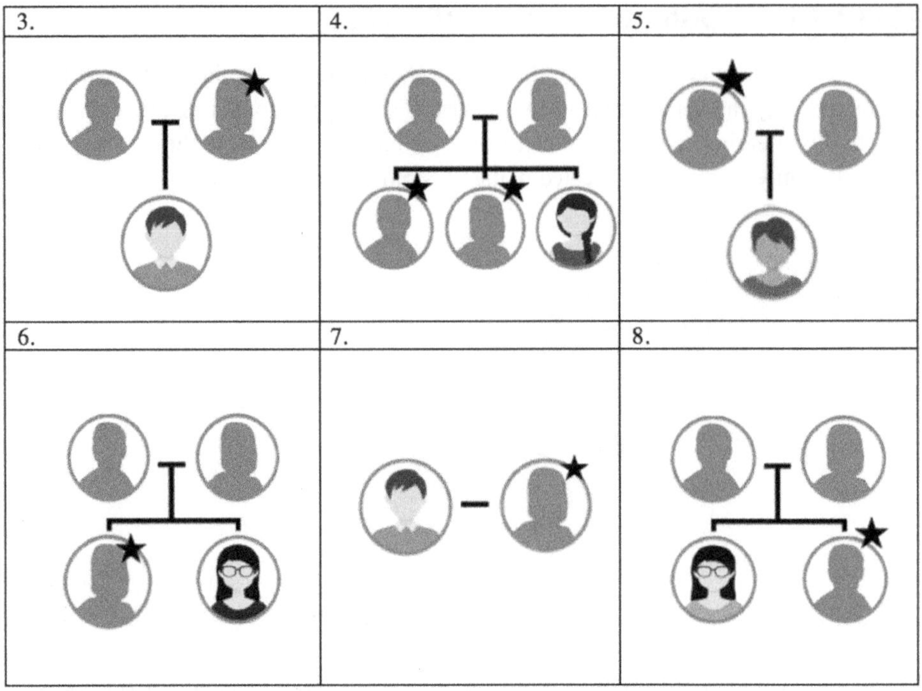

9-3 腕試し Tryout

1. Talk to a Japanese person you know about that person's occupation. Open the conversation by confirming what you already know. Find out what was attractive about that job, and what other jobs, if any, have been considered or pursued before the current one.
2. Participate in a toast.

◆ Scene 9-4 練習 Practice

理解練習 Comprehension practice

9-4-1C Where's the city? (BTS 11)

Amy is asking Takashi about where various cities are located in Japan. Select the location on the map that corresponds to the city they are discussing.

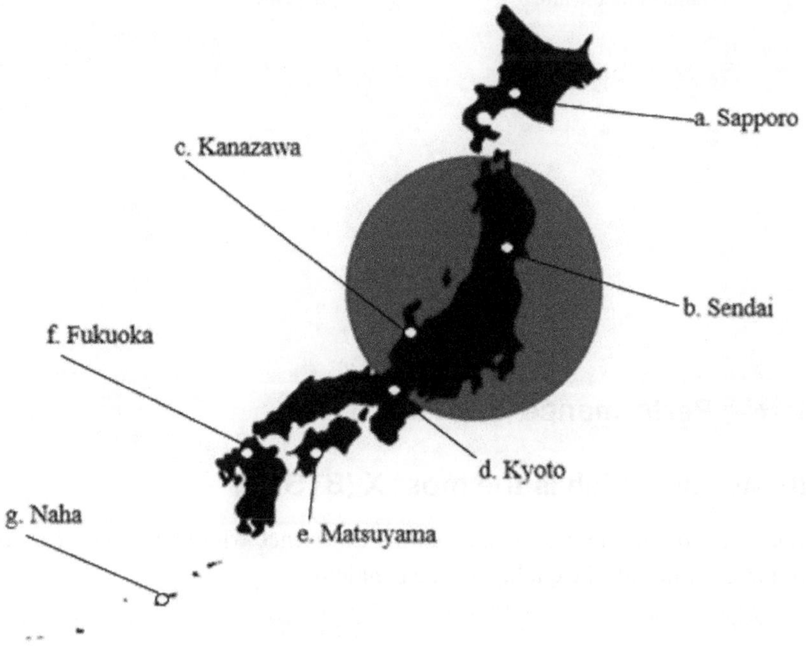

Ex. 1.	c	5.	
2.	e	6.	
3.		7.	
4.			

9-4-2C Which is the most . . . (BTS 10)

In each conversation between Brian and Akie a comparison is made. Select the quality being discussed from the options below, and write what has the most of that quality.

Fastest	Biggest	Hottest	Wants to do the most
Cheapest	Prettiest	Strongest	

	Quality	What has the most
Ex. 1.	Prettiest	The red dress
Ex. 2.	Wants to do the most	Engineer
3.		
4.		
5.		
6.		
7.		

実演練習 Performance practice

9-4-3P Asking which is the most X (BTS 10)

Your colleague, Tomita-san, tells you about his experience with various entities. Ask him which of these entities fits the quality that he mentions.

Ex. 1.

Tomita-san	いろいろなレストランに食べに行きました。どこも美味しかったですよ。	I went to eat at various restaurants. They were all good!
You	一番美味しかったのはどこですか？	Which (lit. where) was the tastiest?

Ex. 2.

Tomita-san	いろいろな時間にバスに乗ってみました。いつも結構空いてましたねえ。	I rode the bus at various times. It was fairly empty the whole time!
You	一番空いていたのはいつですか？	When was it the emptiest?

9-4-4P Acknowledging the defining feature of a place (BTS 11, 12)

You and your friend, Tomoe, are talking about places to visit. When Tomoe mentions a feature of a place, ask if the place is famous for that feature.

Ex. 1.

Tomoe	松山行きたいですね。温泉に行きたい。	We want to go to Matsuyama, don't we. I want to go to a hot spring.
You	ああ、松山って温泉で有名なんですね。	Oh, Matsuyama is famous for hot springs, is it?

Ex. 2.

Tomoe	札幌行きたいですね。雪の中で遊びたい。	We want to go to Sapporo, don't we. I want to play in the snow.
You	ああ、札幌って雪で有名なんですね。	Oh, Sapporo is famous for snow, is it?

9-4 腕試し Tryout

1. Discuss cities that are famous for their association with well-known works of literature, art, people, historical events, industry, etc.
2. Find out which prefecture the Japanese people you know are from. (Review Scene 8-4 for this part). Then, find out more about that prefecture. What is it known for? Are there any hot springs?
3. Learn the name of a prefecture, or a city in that prefecture, that a Japanese person you know has never been to and would like to visit.
4. Ask someone which of three or more items they like the best.
5. Ask someone if they like *onsen* or not. If they do like *onsen*, find out which *onsen* is their favorite among the ones they have been to and why.

◆ Scene 9-5 練習 Practice

理解練習 Comprehension practice

9-5-1C Hobbies

Brian is interviewing various people about their hobbies. Write the hobby(s) and the name of the person who enjoys that hobby.

	Name	Hobby
Ex. 1.	Ai-chan	Singing songs
Ex. 2.	Yuya-kun	Swimming and travel
3.		
4.		
5.		
6.		
7.		

実演練習 Performance practice

9-5-2P Justifying a situation (BTS 13, 14)

In response to your friend's comment, give a reason as a justification for either your action or the current situation, using the most appropriate word from the pool of options. You can use each word once.

Ex. 1.

Friend	あれ?ぜんぜん食べてないね。	What? You haven't eaten at all, have you?
You	だってまずいんだもん。	'Cause it tastes awful!

Ex. 2.

Friend	どうしたの?急にいろいろ話し始めて。	Why? You suddenly start talking about everything.
You	だって思い出したんだもん。	'Cause I remembered it!

思(おも)い出(だ)した	見(み)た	難(むず)しい	まずい	任(まか)せた	終(お)わってた
曇(くも)っている	無理(むり)だ	邪魔(じゃま)だ	習(なら)った		

9-5 腕試し Tryout

Find out what hobbies are enjoyed by the Japanese people you know. Ask related questions to engage the people you are talking to. For example, how long have they been practicing the activity? Make appropriate comments and use appropriate 相槌(あいづち) as you listen.

◆ Scene 9-6 練習 Practice

理解練習 Comprehension practice

9-6-1C Order of events (BTS 15)

Indicate the order of the events by writing "1" next to the first event and "2" next to the second event.

Ex. 1. __1 Studying__ __2 Going home__

Ex. 2. __2 Doing it__ __1 Consulting the teacher__

3. _______ Brewing tea _______ Doing it

4. _______ Going _______ Eating

5. _______ Class finishing _______ Doing it

6. _______ Getting warmer _______ Going

9-6-2C Multiplication (BTS 17)

In each utterance, a multiplication is mentioned. Write what is multiplied under "type," the number of times it is multiplied under "times," and the total number under "total."

	Type	Times	Total
Ex. 1.	Copies	2	100
Ex. 2.	People	3	60
3.			
4.			
5.			
6.			

実演練習 Performance practice

9-6-3P Restating the order of tasks (BTS 15)

When your part-time helper, Tomita-san, offers to do something and then mentions something else to do first, ask her to do both, underscoring the order in which they are to be done.

Ex. 1.

Tomita-san	ここ使いますね?あ、先に片付けましょうか。	I'll use it here, okay? Oh, shall I tidy it up first (ahead of it)?
You	そうですね、じゃあ、片付けてから使ってください。	Yes. So, please tidy it up and then use it for me.

Ex. 2.

Tomita-san	お料理しますね?あ、先にリビング掃除しましょうか。	I'll cook, okay? Oh, shall I clean the living room first (ahead of it)?
You	そうですね、じゃあ、リビング掃除してからお料理してください。	Yes. So, please clean the living room and then cook for me.

9-6-4P Describing a situation in terms of multiples (BTS 17)

Your colleague, Hattori-san, makes a comparison between two situations. Show that you are impressed by restating the current situation in terms of multiples of the previous situation.

Ex. 1.

Hattori-san	札幌まではね、先週は１時間で行ったんですけどね、今週は３時間ぐらいかかりました。	To Sapporo, you know, last week I went in 1 hour, but this week it took 3 hours.
You	ということは、今週は３倍かかったんですか。わあ、すごいですね。	So, that means it took 3 times as long this week? Wow, that's amazing.

Ex. 2.

Hattori-san	出張でね、去年は２つの国に行ったんですけどね、今年は２０ぐらいの国に行きました。	On business trips, you know, last year I went to two countries, but this year I went to about 20 countries.
You	ということは、今年は１０倍の国に行ったんですか。わあ、すごいですね。	So, that means you went to 10 times as many countries this year? Wow, that's amazing.

9-6 腕試し Tryout

1. At an appropriate time give someone a compliment. Respond appropriately to any attempts they make at deflecting the compliment, showing humility, or complimenting in return.
2. When someone offers you a compliment, respond appropriately through such strategies as deflecting the compliment, showing humility, and complimenting/encouraging in return.

◆ Scene 9-7 練習 Practice

読み練習 Reading practice

9-7-1R Discussing schedules

Read the following statements about various schedules.

1. 月曜日に来るのはだれ？
2. だって水曜日はだめなんだもん。
3. どうして土曜日なんですか？
4. え、火曜日にするの？ハヤ！
5. １週間じゃ何にもできないよ。
6. やっぱり木曜日より金曜日がいいな。
7. 日曜日にはもうしてあったよ。
8. 男子も女子も土日がいいって。

Ex. 1. What is said about Monday? Who is coming? ________

Ex. 2. What is said about Tuesday? It's soon. ________

3. What is said about Wednesday? ________
4. What is said about Friday? ________
5. What is said about the boys and girls? ________

9-7-2R Guessing whether it's a yes or no

Based on the following responses to an invitation that you extended for a leisure activity, guess whether what is unsaid is going to be a yes or no.

1. 今週の火曜日はサークルないし、先生も来ないから ……。 Y ✓ N ____
2. 木曜日はだめだし、金曜日はミーティングがあるから ……。 Y ____ N ✓
3. 月曜日は男子はできるけど、女子ができないから ……。 Y ____ N ____
4. 来週からは大学ないし、テストもないから ……。 Y ____ N ____
5. 今週はアメリカから先生が来るし、レポートもあるから ……。 Y ____ N ____
6. 今週は大きなアサイメントもないし、プレゼンもないから Y ____ N ____

書き練習 Writing practice

文字練習 Symbol practice

Use the Symbol Practice sheets in Appendix A to practice kanji characters #34-43 for Scene 9-7.

9-7-3W Which day is it?

Listen to the conversation and write down the day of the event. If mentioned, write down whether it is held this week or next week.

Ex. 1. 火曜日

Ex. 2. 今週の金曜日

3. ______________________

4. ______________________

5. ______________________

◆ Scene 9-8 練習 Practice

読み練習 Reading practice

9-8-1R Discussing duration and height

Read the following statements in text messages and identify the duration or height mentioned.

Ex. 1. 上まで 20 分ぐらい。

Ex. 2. スカイツリーの高さは 634 メートル。

3. タクシーで 30 分ぐらいのところ。
4. 川上さんのオフィスから5分ぐらいのところにある。
5. 高校まであと1、2分だよ。
6. ギザの大ピラミッドの高さは 147 メートルって聞きましたよ。
7. 日本に行くのに12時間 30 分かかる。
8. 高さ300メートル!?エッフェルタワーって高っ!

Ex. 1. twenty minutes______ Ex. 2. 634 meters______ 3. ______

4. ______ 5. ______ 6. ______

7. ______ 8. ______

9-8-2R Discussing occupations

Read the following statements about people's occupations.

1. 川上さんはITのフリーランスです。
2. 一つ下のオフィスでシステムエンジニアをしています。
3. アメリカの高校で日本語の先生をしております。
4. あの男の子は来年から高校生になるんだって。
5. 今から来年のインターンのこと聞きに行って来るね。
6. あの人名前が分からないけど、スペイン語の先生してるって聞いたよ。
7. 学生の３分の２が男子で、３分の１が女子なんだって。
8. 名前とメールアドレスはセーブしてありますよ。

Ex. 1. Where does the system engineer work? In the office one floor below______

Ex. 2. What has been saved? Names and email addresses______

3. Where does the Japanese teacher work? ____________________

4. Who is the IT freelancer? ____________________

5. What is the ratio of boys and girls among students? ____________________

書き練習 Writing practice

文字練習 Symbol practice

Use the Symbol Practice sheets in Appendix A to practice kanji characters 44-52 for Scene 9-8.

9-8-3W Identifying names of people, high schools, and colleges

Read the following names and write whether they are the names of people, high schools, or colleges.

Ex. 1. テキサステック　大学の名前

Ex. 2. アブラハム・リンカーン　人の名前

3. マーケット・シニア・ハイスクール ____________________

4. ミシガンステイト ____________________

5. トーマス・エジソン ____________________

6. ロッキーマウンテン・ハイ ____________________

7. オハイオステイト ____________________

8. カズオ・イシグロ ____________________

9-8-4W Writing time duration

Listen to the audio and write down the duration of each activity or event.

Ex. 1. ３０分

Ex. 2. ３時間３０分

3. ____________________

4. ____________________

5. ____________________

6. ____________________

◆ Scene 9-9 練習 Practice

読み練習 Reading practice

9-9-1R Introduction

Read the following introductory statements and fill in the table with the appropriate information.

Ex. 1. オハイオ州立大学の木下です。どうぞよろしく。

Ex. 2. 上のフロアでＩＴのサポートをしている村上といいます。よろしくお願いします。

3. JLCの山本でございます。これからよろしくお願いいたします。

4. 中国から来ましたリーといいます。今日からよろしくお願いします。

5. 四国大学の村上です。今年もどうぞよろしくお願いします。

6. どうも。ポートランド州立大学の山中といいます。一週間よろしくお願いします。

7. サイエンスクラブの川下です。前にも来たことがありますが、今日もよろしくお願いします。

	Name	From (place or affiliation)
Ex. 1.	Kinoshita	The Ohio State University
Ex. 2.	Murakami	IT support upstairs
3.		
4.		
5.		
6.		
7.		

9-9-2R Identifying the one

Read the following descriptions and connect names with descriptions below. The lists include descriptions and names that you won't be matching with anything.

Ex. 1. ジェームスよりもっと前に立っているのがケイトです。

Ex. 2. 上からじゃなくて下から来たのがジェイソンです。

3. 上のクラスの男の学生がウィルソンさんです。

4. 木曜も金曜も来なかったのがウィリアムズさんです。
5. ３年前まで中国に行っていたのがジェレマイアさんです。
6. 山下先生の学生で、川上さんの友だちなのがキンバリーさんです。
7. 九州の高校のことを聞いていたのがエイミーさんです。
8. 村山さんの下の名前を聞いていたのがエミリーさんです。
9. 下のクラスだけどすごくよくできる女の学生がキャシーです。

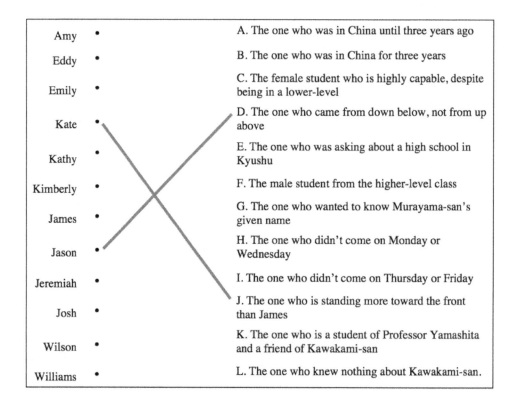

Amy •	A. The one who was in China until three years ago
Eddy •	B. The one who was in China for three years
Emily •	C. The female student who is highly capable, despite being in a lower-level
Kate •	D. The one who came from down below, not from up above
Kathy •	E. The one who was asking about a high school in Kyushu
Kimberly •	F. The male student from the higher-level class
James •	G. The one who wanted to know Murayama-san's given name
Jason •	H. The one who didn't come on Monday or Wednesday
Jeremiah •	I. The one who didn't come on Thursday or Friday
Josh •	J. The one who is standing more toward the front than James
Wilson •	K. The one who is a student of Professor Yamashita and a friend of Kawakami-san
Williams •	L. The one who knew nothing about Kawakami-san.

9-9-3R Discussing plans

Read the following statements about plans and identify the time frame being mentioned.

Ex. 1. 大学に行ってからそちらに行きますね。
Ex. 2. 来月のことで先生に聞いてみたいことってありますか？
3. 川村先生に聞いてからのほうがいいよ。
4. 山下さんが来てからみんなで行きましょう
5. 来週行ってみたいところはありますか？

6. スケジュールが分かってからメールしますね。
7. ビールは大人になってからですよ。
8. 高校の先生になってからやってみたいことってありますか。

Ex. 1.	After going to college	Ex. 2.	Next month
3.	__________	4.	__________
5.	__________	6.	__________
7.	__________	8.	__________

書き練習 Writing practice

文字練習 Symbol practice

Use the Symbol Practice sheets in Appendix A to practice kanji characters #53-58 for Scene 9-9.

9-9-4W Writing down names

Listen to a voice mail addressed to your colleague, Sato-san, and write down the last name of the person and also the name of the school.

Ex. 1
四国大学の
中山さんから
お電話がありました。

Ex. 2.
オハイオ州立大学の
村上さんから
お電話がありました。

3.
__________の
__________さんから
お電話がありました。

4.
__________の
__________さんから
お電話がありました。

5.
__________の
__________さんから
お電話がありました。

6.
__________の
__________さんから
お電話がありました。

◆ 評価 Assessment

Answer sheet templates are provided in Appendix B for the Assessment sections.

聞いてみよう Listening comprehension

Read the context, listen to the audio, and then answer the questions based on what you hear. If you hear something unfamiliar, focus on what you know to determine the correct answer.

1. Yagi-bucho and Kanda-san are looking at a new poster for a promotion.
   a. What does Yagi-san want to know?
   b. What does she then say she likes about the poster?
   c. How does Kanda-san describe his own abilities? Be specific.
2. Amy and her fellow part-time co-worker have been cleaning up a room together.
   a. What does Amy say they did?
   b. How far along are they, according to her co-worker?
   c. What wrong assumption did Amy have?
   d. What actually is the situation?
3. Yagi-san and everybody on her project team have gone out after work.
   a. What has Yagi-san taken everyone out to show appreciation for?
   b. What does Yagi-san invite everybody to do after the toast?
4. Kanda-san just called his wife on his cell phone.
   a. Why does Kanda-san apologize?
   b. What does he ask his wife to do?
5. Takashi saw Amy playing a video game and started talking to her.
   a. Describe Amy's status with regard to her paper.
   b. What is Takashi's concern?
   c. What question does Takashi ask himself?
6. Takashi ran into Amy again two days later, the day when the report is due.
   a. What aspect of Amy's work impresses Takashi?
   b. What comparison does Takashi make between Amy and Takashi?
   c. What explanation does Takashi offer?
7. Suzuki-san is meeting Mr. Subaru Ikegami, who is a potential marriage partner, and is asking about his work.
   a. What type of place does Ikegami-san work for?
   b. What does Subaru do there?
   c. What does he not do?

8. Suzuki-san and Ikegami-san continue their conversation, asking about each other's background.
   a. What cities does Ikegami-san mention by name that he has lived in before Kyoto?
   b. How does he explain the large number of places he has lived?
   c. What does Ikegami-san say about Kanazawa?
   d. What does Suzuki-san want to know about Sendai?
9. Now Suzuki-san and Ikegami-san are talking about their hobbies.
   a. What is Ikegami-san's hobby?
   b. What common feeling about their respective hobbies do the two share? Why do they feel this way?
   c. What occasional issue does Ikegami-san bring up?
   d. How does he resolve it?
10. Kanda-san is helping his wife locate something at home.
   a. What is Mrs. Kanda looking for?
   b. Where has she looked?
   c. How does Kanda-san deduce its location?
   d. What concern do they have?

使ってみよう Dry run

For each of the following, listen to the audio and respond to what was said based on the context.

1. You are speaking to an office associate. You are going to go do the activity mentioned (a) in the late afternoon today; (b) tonight; (c) every week; (d) the next academic term; (e) during spring break.
2. You are speaking to a friend about other friends' hobbies. Tell him that (a) Yuta's hobby is probably music; (b) Sakura's hobby is probably reading; (c) Yui's hobby is probably gaming; (d) Yamato's hobby is probably jazz music; (e) Shota's hobby, you think, is cooking; (f) Lynn's hobby, you think, is (visiting) hot springs.
3. You are speaking to an office associate, who is wondering about your common acquaintance, Sugita-kun. Disclose to her that he was (a) an engineer for 2 to 3 years; (b) a full-time short-term employee for as many as 10 years; (c) a public servant for just 10 months; (d) an attorney for at least 2 to 3 decades; (e) a company employee for a long time; (f) doing education-related work for 5 to 6 years.
4. You are speaking to someone whom you just met at a reception. He seems interested in New Orleans. Tell him that it is famous for jazz. Moreover, the food is tasty.
5. You are speaking to a new intern at the intern orientation. He asks you about Yabe-san, the section chief. Tell him that she is a great (admirable) person. She is very knowledgeable about IT-related matters, and she is interested in games, too.

6. When asked by a *senpai* if you will do something, respond that you will first (a) study and then do it; (b) talk to the teacher and then do it; (c) eat and then do it; (d) do a toast and then do it; (e) finish reading about two-thirds of this and then do it.
7. When a friend asks you why, explain in a way that shows you aren't taking much responsibility and feel that your action is justified because (a) you forgot; (b) it was delicious; (c) you like *onsen*; (d) no one cleans up.
8. You just received an email from a co-worker about next week. When your *senpai* asks about next Tuesday, respond that it says (lit. it is written) that it seems it will be (lit. become) about 50 people.

Now it's your turn to start the conversation based on the given context. Listen to how the other person reacts to you. For some items, you may not get a verbal response. Don't be concerned if you hear things you have not yet learned.

9. Ask a *senpai* which of the rooms near the elevator on the third floor she thinks seems to be the easiest to use.
10. Ask a *koohai* who it is that (a) threw out the trash here; (b) redid (lit. did new) next week's schedule; (c) is singing songs in the next room; (d) drew this amazingly beautiful picture.
11. You are speaking to a senior student. Show her your admiration with a bunch of "why" questions, using どうして (rather than なんで). Ask her (a) why she is interested in law; (b) why she knows so much about hot springs; (c) why her French pronunciation is so good; (d) why she can organize things so well; (e) why she is so good at singing; (f) why her office is always so tidy.
12. You are speaking to a senior member of your group. Ask him questions related to things that you feel critically about. Use なぜ or どうして for these. Ask (a) why he always starts the laundry at such late hours; (b) why he never cleans his own room; (c) why he doesn't study before exams; (d) why he doesn't ever think, then speak; (e) why he always looks busy and doesn't relax even a little; (f) why he doesn't wash (things) more thoroughly (cleanly); (g) why he makes decisions so rapidly and by himself?
13. You are speaking to a supervisor. Ask him if it's all right for you to explain the legal matters to the part-time workers.
14. You are giving a presentation about language use among students at a Japanese college in the 2010's and explaining figures in a set of pie charts. State that (a) 80% of students use such forms as「はや!」、「うま!」、「おもしろ!」almost every day; (b) But that only two-thirds of them use「やば!」; (c) And that there are twice as many male students who use「まじ」as female students.
15. A teacher assigned a novel to read in class yesterday, and a friend has just told you that he finished reading the entire book already. Express your shock and amazement that he did it so fast.
16. You have entered a room that is very messy. Express your frustration that no one cleans up this room.

読んでみよう Contextualized reading

Read the information and answer the questions that follow.

(1) Here is the upcoming schedule of guest speakers for JLC at Clinton College.

日付	ゲスト	場所
1月１７日(木) １４時半〜１６時	川村先生(九州大学) 「ビジネス日本語：コミュニケーションマナー」	リンカーンホール ２０１
3月２２日(金) 9時〜１０時４５分	山下先生(四国大学) 「インターンシップ：日本語とグローバリゼーション」	フレンドホール １８０

Part 1.

a. What is the title and name of the guest speaker on January 17? Where is she from?
b. On what day is the lecture? From what time to what time? Where is it?
c. What is the topic of her lecture?

Part 2.

a. What is the title and name of the guest speaker on March 22? Where is he from?
b. On what day is the lecture? From what time to what time? Where is it?
c. What is the topic of his lecture?

(2) An email from your colleague:

Subject: ディナーセッション
来週の火曜日から、シンガポール国立大学のジョーンズ先生のレクチャーがありますね。前日の月曜日にサンフラワーというところで１８時からディナーセッションがあるのですが、よかったら来ませんか？ 中国語のメニューもありますけど、中国語分かりますか?. 木下

a. What is the name of your colleague?
b. When is the lecture? Who is giving the lecture? Where is the lecturer from?
c. What invitation is made? Provide details.
d. What additional question is asked? Why?

書き取り Dictation

Listen, imagine the context, repeat silently what you hear, then write it down.

1. ______________________________。
2. ______________________________。
3. ______________________________。
4. ______________________________。
5. ______________________________。
6. ______________________________。
7. ______________________________。
8. ______________________________。

書いてみよう Contextualized writing

Compose a note according to the directions.

1. Leave a memo to your colleague that you will go and ask Dr. Nakamura's schedule for Friday this week.

2. Write an announcement about the schedule change: The lecture on 1/17 (next Thursday) starts at 12:45.

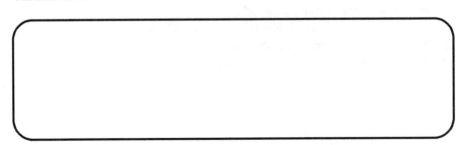

3. Tell your colleague about the lecture by Dr. Kawakami of Portland State University next Wednesday. Invite your colleague to a workshop that will be held the day before (Tuesday) from 5:15 p.m.

知ってる? What do you know?

Select the most appropriate option and write the letter on your answer sheet.

1. You've been asked to describe your new school.
   留学生(りゅうがくせい)______多(おお)い______学校(がっこう)です。(BTS 1)
   a. が•の
   b. は•の
   c. の•Ø
2. You've been asked about the new part-timer worker.
   日本語(にほんご)______すごく上手(じょうず)________人(ひと)ですよ。(BTS 1)
   a. が•な
   b. は•な
   c. が•の
3. You ask who it is that apologized.
   謝(あやま)った____は誰(だれ)ですか。(BTS 2)
   a. の
   b. な
   c. こと
4. You tell your friend that you enjoy cleaning up your apartment.
   アパート掃除(そうじ)する______好(す)きですよ。(BTS 2)
   a. の
   b. な
   c. こと

5. Noun の can be used to make ____________. (BTS 2)

   a. a minor sentence into a major sentence

   b. a sentence into a noun

   c. an unknown noun into a known one

6. You've been asked if the meeting room has been straightened up by someone. Without mentioning who did it, you reply:

   はい、あの会議室は________________________。(BTS 3)

   a. 片付けてあります

   b. 掃除しています

   c. 片付けていました

7. You've been asked about an incident two weeks ago. You tell your classmate that at that time at least everything had been put in order:

   あの時は整理__________んだ。(BTS 3)

   a. してある

   b. していた

   c. してあった

8. Your homestay mother wonders who has been throwing the garbage out every day. You reply:

   私が______________んですけど ……。(BTS 3)

   a. 捨ててある

   b. 捨てている

   c. 捨てた

9. You're feeling rather frustrated by the mess your roommate left in the kitchen. You say: (BTS 4, 16)

   a. とんでもない!

   b. ハヤ!

   c. まったく!

10. You've been asked why you're going to the library. You reply:

    本を____________行きます。(BTS 5, 15)

    a. 借りて

    b. 借りに

    c. 借りてから

11. Two-thirds in Japanese is ________. (BTS 6)

    a. 三分の二

    b. 二分の三

    c. 2点3

12. You've been asked why you're so upset. You reply:
試験が全然ダメ______________。(BTS 8)
    a. のだった
    b. だったんだ
    c. からだ
13. What is the difference between using particles し and から to express reason? (BTS 9)
    a. から implies that there's more than one reason whereas し puts the focus on only one reason.
    b. し implies that there's more than one reason whereas から offers only one reason.
    c. し follows a complete sentence whereas から follows a noun.
14. You use ______ to express "the most X" when comparing three or more items. (BTS 10)
    a. もっと
    b. ほう
    c. 一番
15. How many 県 'prefectures' are there in Japan? (BTS 11)
    a. 41
    b. 43
    c. 47
16. When entering an *onsen* to bathe, you must first _______. (BTS 12)
    a. soak in the hot-spring water
    b. cover yourself with a small towel
    c. wash yourself at a washing station
17. It is appropriate to use だって at the beginning of a sentence when you are _______about something. (BTS 13)
    a. angry with someone
    b. seriously concerned
    c. offering an excuse
18. You've been asked when you're going to practice aikido. You reply:
宿題___________練習する。(BTS 15)
    a. したから
    b. してから
    c. していて
19. You tell your roommate that you'll go and listen to music (and return).
ちょっと音楽__________くる。(BTS 15)
    a. 聞いて
    b. 聞いたから
    c. 聞いてから

20. You've been asked why you were given a free ticket. You reply:
ちゃんと___________、くれたんだ。(BTS 15)

a. 答(こた)えたけど

b. 答(こた)えてから

c. 答(こた)えたから

21. You complain that even though you studied ten times harder than your friend, you still couldn't do well.

１０____も勉強(べんきょう)したけど、できなかったんだ。(BTS 17)

a. 度(ど)

b. 倍(ばい)

c. 回(かい)

22. Square brackets「 」are used in Japanese for ________. (BTL 1)

a. emphasis

b. proper Nouns

c. quotations

23. A small っ at the end of a Japanese word or phrase indicates that the ________. (BTL 2)

a. sound is cut off abruptly

b. sentence is unfinished

c. speaker/writer is uncertain

24. Japanese uses Chinese elements ________. (BTL 3)

a. to create technical vocabulary

b. only for borrowed Chinese vocabulary

c. to substitute for English borrowings

第 10 幕
Act 10

次回、頑張ろう。

(じかい、がんば)

Let’s do our best next time.

◆ Scene 10-1 練習 Practice

理解練習 Comprehension practice

10-1-1C Doing what in advance? (BTS 1)

In some of the exchanges you hear, one of the speakers mentions doing something in advance. What activity is mentioned? Indicate the appropriate action from the selection provided; or, if no advance activity is mentioned, write "none." You will not use all of the selections. You will use a selection only once.

Ex. 1. __j__   Ex. 2. __none__   3. ______   4. ______
5. ______   6. ______   7. ______   8. ______

a. attend a meeting	b. buy tickets	c. check and see	d. eat	e. make copies
f. practice	g. recommend	h. request	i. save	j. sleep
k. study	l. tidy things up	m. travel	n. write down	

10-1-2C What activities are suggested? (BTS 2)

Listen to the exchanges between friends and determine what activities are suggested. Select from the illustrations provided.

Ex. 1. __d__   Ex. 2. __j__   3. ______   4. ______
5. ______   6. ______   7. ______   8. ______
9. ______   10. ______

実演練習 Performance practice

10-1-3P Reassuring that everything will be fine (BTS 1, 3)

When your supervisor, Yoshida-san, asks you to do something, reassure her that you will do it today to be ready for a later date.

Ex. 1.

Yoshida-san	この実験のレポート、書いてくれませんか。	Will you write the report for this experiment for me?
You	わかりました。今日書いておきますので。	OK. I'll write it today, so it'll be fine.

Ex. 2.

Yoshida-san	申し訳ないのですが、鈴木さんに謝っていただけませんか。	I'm sorry to trouble you, but would you apologize to Suzuki-san?
You	わかりました。今日謝っておきますので。	OK. I'll apologize to her today, so it'll be fine.

10-1-4P Let's do it! (BTS 2)

When a friend asks if you will do something, respond with "let's do it."

Ex. 1.

Ikeda-kun	行く?	Are we going to go?
You	うん、行こう!	Yeah, let's go!

Ex. 2.

Ikeda-kun	聞いてみる?	Are we going to ask?
You	うん、聞いてみよう!	Yeah, let's ask!

10-1 腕試し Tryout

By engaging in small talk about what a Japanese friend or co-worker likes to do, find out how to say in Japanese the name of some spectator sports (hockey, gymnastics, swimming, etc.) or stage performances that you might like to go see.

◆ Scene 10-2 練習 Practice

理解練習 Comprehension practice

10-2-1C In the middle of… (BTS 4)

Listen to each statement and classify the noun with 中(ちゅう•じゅう) as referring to (a) an activity that happens throughout the whole time span; (b) an activity that happens by the end of the time span; (c) being in the middle of an activity (and thus unable to do something else).

Ex. 1.	☐ a	☒ b	☐ c
Ex. 2.	☐ a	☐ b	☒ c
3.	☐ a	☐ b	☐ c
4.	☐ a	☐ b	☐ c
5.	☐ a	☐ b	☐ c
6.	☐ a	☐ b	☐ c
7.	☐ a	☐ b	☐ c
8.	☐ a	☐ b	☐ c

10-2-2C I'm so sorry. (BTS 5)

Listen to each statement of apology and mark all of the elements that are present: (a) statement of apology; (b) description of the situation; (c) explanation; (d) intention to remedy things in the future.

Ex. 1.	☒ a	☒ b	☐ c	☐ d
Ex. 2.	☒ a	☒ b	☐ c	☒ d
3.	☐ a	☐ b	☐ c	☐ d
4.	☐ a	☐ b	☐ c	☐ d
5.	☐ a	☐ b	☐ c	☐ d
6.	☐ a	☐ b	☐ c	☐ d
7.	☐ a	☐ b	☐ c	☐ d
8.	☐ a	☐ b	☐ c	☐ d

実演練習 Performance practice

10-2-3P Suggesting (BTS 4)

When Endo-san, your teammate who is junior to you, suggests a time frame for doing a task, suggest that you do it by the end of that time frame.

Ex. 1.

Endo-san	これ、今日仕上げましょうか。	Shall we finish this up today?
You	そうだね。今日中に仕上げよう。	Yes, let's finish it up by the end of today.

Ex. 2.

Endo-san	今週もう一度実験しましょうか。	Shall we do the experiment one more time this week?
You	そうだね。今週中に実験しよう。	Yes, let's do the experiment by the end of this week.

10-2-4P Apologizing (BTS 5)

Your teacher, Kato-sensei, notices an issue. Take responsibility and apologize, then promise to do it right away.

Ex. 1.

Kato-sensei	ファイル、誰も整理してないですね。	No one has sorted the files, have they.
You	もっと早く整理しなくてすみませんでした。すぐ整理しますから。	Sorry for not sorting them sooner. I'll sort them right away.

Ex. 2.

Kato-sensei	作文、1ページも書いてないですね。	You haven't written a page of your composition, have you.
You	もっと早く書かなくてすみませんでした。すぐ書きますから。	Sorry for not writing it sooner. I'll write it right away.

10-2 腕試し Tryout

Ask some Japanese friends if they like going to sporting events, plays, etc. and see if they might like to go in a certain time frame (i.e., this week, this month, etc.). Depending on their response, determine who will arrange to buy the tickets or discuss what is keeping them busy.

◆ Scene 10-3 練習 Practice

理解練習 Comprehension practice

10-3-1C What's going on? (BTS 6)

Select the situation that corresponds to what the speaker says. You will use each description only once.

Ex. 1. __a__ Ex. 2. __f__ 3.____ 4.____ 5.____ 6. ____

a. A hostess at a restaurant is greeting a customer.
b. A visiting professional is making a request of her host.
c. A university student is asking another student about a mutual acquaintance.
d. A customer is asking a salesperson at a store a question.
e. A representative of Aoi Shuppan is asking for someone at the office reception desk.
f. An intern is consulting her boss.

10-3-2C What did they order?

Listen to each exchange and write down what the man orders.

Ex. 1. Another beer, small size______ Ex. 2. Grilled meat combo__________
3. ____________________ 4. ____________________
5. ____________________ 6. ____________________
7. ____________________ 8. ____________________

実演練習 Performance practice

10-3-3P Confirming positions (BTS 6)

You are attending a reception. When a client of yours inquires about someone she recognizes, assure her that she is right, using the appropriate politeness level, and provide the name according to the illustrations. The illustrations show whether the person under discussion belongs to your in-group or not.

Ex. 1.

Client	社長さんですか？	Is that the president?
You	はい、社長の立花でございます。	Yes, it's President Tachibana.

Ex. 2.

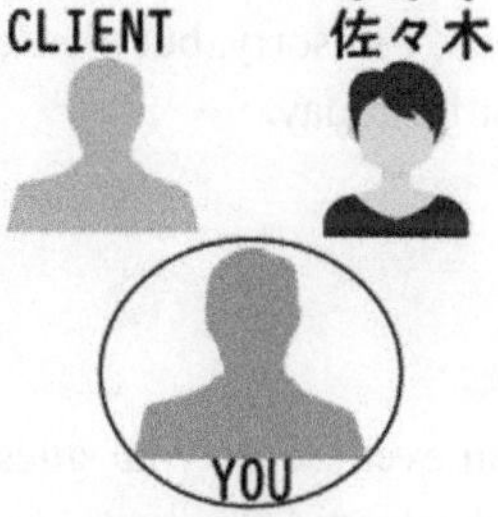

Client	学長さんですか？	Is that the school president?
You	はい、学長の佐々木さんでいらっしゃいます。	Yes, it's President Sasaki.

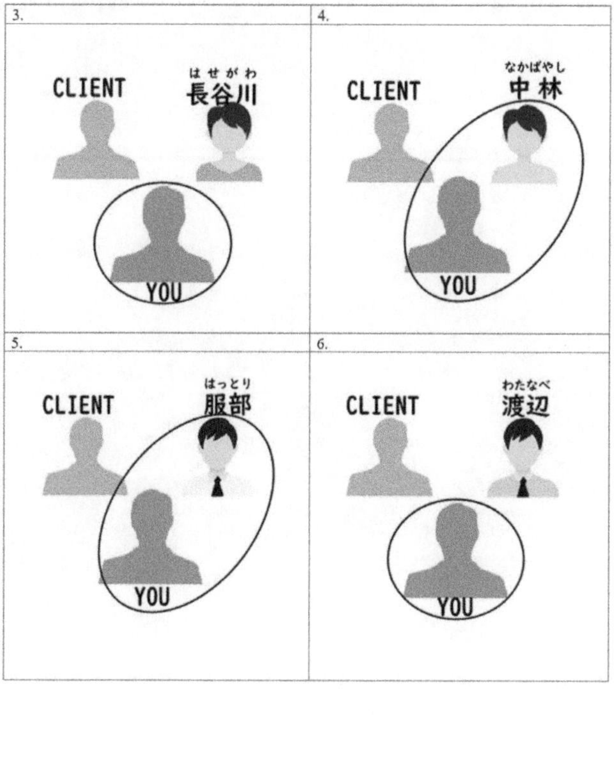

10-3-4P Requesting politely (BTS 6)

When a client suggests that he does something (for you), take him up on the offer with an apology for the trouble and show your intention to minimize the imposition.

Ex. 1.

Client	あと１週間待ちましょうか。	Why don't I wait for one more week?
You	では、申し訳ありませんが、あと１週間だけお待ちください。	Then, I'm sorry, but please wait for just one more week.

Ex. 2.

Client	今日は遠慮しましょうか？	Why don't I hold back today?
You	では、申し訳ありませんが、今日だけご遠慮ください。	Then, I'm sorry, but please hold back just for today.

10-3 腕試し Tryout

When you are hosting someone, either at home or at an event, urge your guests politely to engage in various activities: to enter, to sit, to not hold back, and to relax.

◆ Scene 10-4 練習 Practice

理解練習 Comprehension practice

10-4-1C How certain? (BTS 8)

Listen to each statement and indicate if the speaker is marking what she says as (a) a statement of fact; (b) a strong conjecture; or (c) an uncertainty. If you hear something unfamiliar, rely on what you know to choose the correct answer.

Ex. 1.	a. fact	(b.) strong conjecture	c. uncertainty
Ex. 2.	a. fact	b. strong conjecture	(c.) uncertainty
3.	a. fact	b. strong conjecture	c. uncertainty
4.	a. fact	b. strong conjecture	c. uncertainty
5.	a. fact	b. strong conjecture	c. uncertainty
6.	a. fact	b. strong conjecture	c. uncertainty
7.	a. fact	b. strong conjecture	c. uncertainty
8.	a. fact	b. strong conjecture	c. uncertainty

実演練習 Performance practice

10-4-2P Gently disagreeing (BTS 8)

Your *senpai*, Gotō-san, makes some outrageous statements. Gently suggest that the opposite situation might actually be the case.

Ex. 1.

Gotō-san	川野くんが通訳するんだって。絶対無理だよね、それ。	I hear that Kawano-kun is going to interpret. That's absolutely impossible, right?
You	無理じゃないかもしれませんよ。	It might not be impossible, you know.

Ex. 2.

Gotō-san	これ間違えてる人、絶対いないよね？	People who got this wrong, there absolutely aren't any, right?
You	いるかもしれませんよ。	There might be some, you know.

◆ Scene 10-5 練習 Practice

理解練習 Comprehension practice

10-5-1C How is self-image restored? (BTS 10)

Kanda-san is talking to an intern who is apologizing about a job not well done. What does the intern apologize about and what promise does she make to restore her self-image in response to Kanda-san's encouragement?

	The issue	The promise for the next time
Ex. 1.	Completely wrong translation	Research more carefully
Ex. 2.	Bad performance on presentation	Practice more in advance
3.		
4.		
5.		
6.		
7.		

実演練習 Performance practice

10-5-2P Acknowledging the workload (BTS 9)

Sakata-san, who is a part-time worker under your supervision, is checking what she is expected to do. Confirm her assumption, while showing your appreciation for the amount of work she is having to do.

Ex. 1.

Sakata-san	こちらのは全部翻訳するんですね？	These over here, I'm to translate all of them, right?
You	翻訳することが多くて悪いけど、よろしく。	I'm sorry that there is a lot to translate, but please do.

Ex. 2.

Sakata-san	歌舞伎の切符もお弁当も買っておくんですね？	Kabuki tickets and boxed lunches, I'm to buy them in advance, right?
You	買っておくものが多くて悪いけど、よろしく。	I'm sorry that there are a lot to buy in advance, but please do.

◆ Scene 10-6 練習 Practice

理解練習 Comprehension practice

10-6-1C What is being described? (BTS 9)

Listen to each statement and indicate what the speaker is describing and how he is describing it.

	What is being described	Description
Ex. 1.	The biggest weakness	Waking up early in the morning
Ex. 2.	What made him happy this year	Passing the exam for the university that he absolutely wanted to get into
3.	______	______
4.	______	______
5.	______	______
6.	______	______
7.	______	______

10-6-2C Who has more? (BTS 12)

Select from the options below and write the quality being discussed. Then mark the option that has more of that quality. There are expressions you have not yet studied. You should still be able to gather the necessary information, using the Japanese you already know.

Ex. 1.	Better English	☐ Tanaka-san	☒ Sasha
Ex. 2.	More points	☒ The speaker	☐ Ichiro-kun
3.	______	☐ The speaker	☐ Ai-san
4.	______	☐ This year	☐ Last year
5.	______	☐ Today	☐ Last week

6. ______________________ ☐ This month ☐ Last month

7. ______________________ ☐ The speaker ☐ Yamazaki-san

More points	Better at English	Colder	Worse Japanese score
Better at golf	Better at aikido	Knows more foreign languages	

実演練習 Performance practice

10-6-3P Suggesting (BTS 12)

Your friend, Akina, makes a comparison between two alternatives. Agree and rephrase her suggestion as a statement of what it would be better to do.

Ex. 1.

Akina	テストの前にも一生懸命勉強するけど、毎日予習とか復習するのも大切だね。	I study hard before tests, too, but it's also important to preview and review every day, isn't it.
You	そうだね。毎日予習とか復習した方がいいよね。	That's right. Yeah, it's better to preview and review every day, isn't it.

Ex. 2.

Akina	毎日果物を食べてるけど、一番いいのは、夜じゃなく朝食べることなんだって。	I eat fruit every day, but I heard that the best thing is to eat it in the morning, not at night.
You	そうだね。朝食べた方がいいよね。	That's right. Yeah, it's better to eat it in the morning, isn't it.

10-6-4P Being at a loss as to how (BTS 13)

When your friend, Eita, suggests that the two of you do something, agree, but tell him that you can't figure out how.

Ex. 1.

Eita	このアプリ、使おう。	Let's use this app.
You	うん。あ、でも使い方分からないよ。	OK. Oh, but I don't know how to use it.

Ex. 2.

Eita	これ、もうちょっと分析しよう。	Let's analyze this a little more.
You	うん。あ、でも分析のし方分からないよ。	OK. Oh, but I don't know how to analyze it.

◆ Scene 10-7 練習 Practice

読み練習 Reading practice

10-7-1R Doing things ahead of time

Read the following statements and write down in English what things are (going to be) done ahead of time. Provide a reason and indicate whether it is perceived as an explanation or a direct cause.

Ex. 1. 時間がないので、みんなからのリクエストを先に聞いておきました。
Ex. 2. いいアイディアだからメモに書いておこうよ。
3. 金曜日は新しい先生が見えるので、10時半までには来ておきますね。
4. ３時からは人が多くなるので、先にトイレに行っておいてください。
5. 来週は忙しくなりそうだから、このリスト、今週中に見ておいてくださいませんか？

	Things (to be) done ahead of time	Reason	Explanation or direct cause?	
Ex 1.	Ask for everyone's request	There's no time	☒ explanatory	☐ direct cause
Ex 2.	Write on a memo	It is a good idea	☐ explanatory	☒ direct cause
3.	______	______	☐ explanatory	☐ direct cause
4.	______	______	☐ explanatory	☐ direct cause
5.	______	______	☐ explanatory	☐ direct cause

10-7-2R What does he suggest?

Read the following text message statements that a friend sent you and write down in English what he suggests.

Ex. 1. もう少し待とうよ。 wait a little longer
Ex. 2. 来週見に行こうね。 go see something next week
3. 先週のこと、新聞に書こうかな。 ______
4. 行ってみようかな、あの新しいレストラン。 ______
5. 英子さんにも聞いてみようね。 ______
6. 時々英語でメールしようよ。 ______

書き練習 Writing practice

文字練習 Symbol practice

Use the Symbol Practice sheets in Appendix A to practice kanji characters # 59–67 for Scene 10-7.

10-7-3W Describing recipes

Listen to the conversation and write a general description of recipes discussed at a cooking class on each day of the week.

クッキングクラススケジュール

月	Ex. 1. 新しい	レシピ
火		レシピ
水		レシピ
木		レシピ
金		レシピ
土		レシピ
日	Ex. 2. 英語で書いてある	レシピ

◆ Scene 10-8 練習 Practice

読み練習 Reading practice

10-8-1R Who is being more polite?

Read the following dialogue transcriptions and circle the name of the person who is being more polite. If both parties are being extra polite, then circle both names. Underline expressions that are extra polite.

Ex. 1.	金田 村上	ここのラーメンレシピはお好きですか? うん、好きだよ。明日も食べたいねえ。
Ex. 2.	田村 国立	今年はどんなものをお買いでしょうか? そうですね。去年のものがまだございますから……。
3.	カスタマー ウェイター	食後にデザートも食べたいんですけど、メニューってありますか? はい、少々お待ちください……。お待たせいたしました。こちらが今日のメニューでございます。
4.	田中 山上	山上さんでいらっしゃいますか? はい、山上でございます。よろしくお願いいたします。
5.	カスタマー バーテンダー	これちょっと飲んでみたいと思ってるんだけど……。 スペシャルドリンクでございますね。かしこまりました。
6.	ミラー 山田	これ、よろしければ今日中にやっておいてくださいませんか? あれ?昨日の午前中にはできていたと思ったのですが……。
7.	学生 先生	昨日はテスト中にやかましくてもうしわけありませんでした。 もういいから。明日のテストの時はあんまりうるさくしないでね。
8.	英子 デボラ	分かったと思います。 英子さん、もうお分かりですか?さすがですね。

10-8-2R Is Sasha certain?

Based on the text message exchanges you read, indicate the level of certainty Sasha demonstrates: certain, tentative, or skeptical?

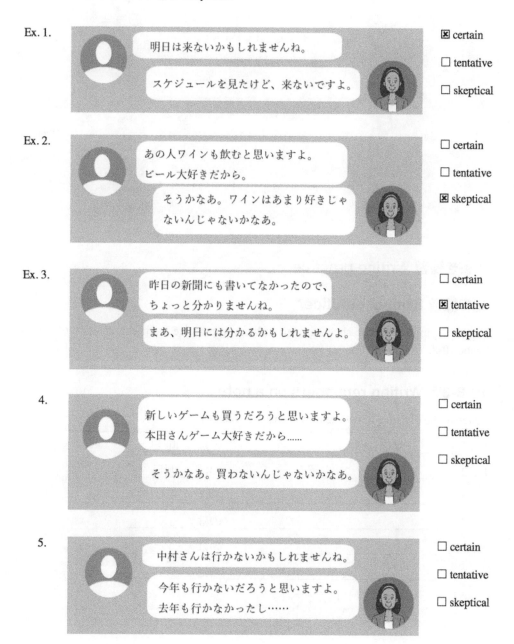

Ex. 1.

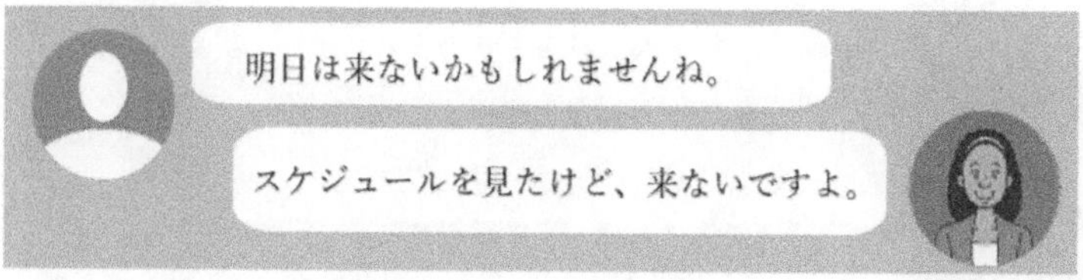
明日は来ないかもしれませんね。
スケジュールを見たけど、来ないですよ。

☒ certain
☐ tentative
☐ skeptical

Ex. 2.

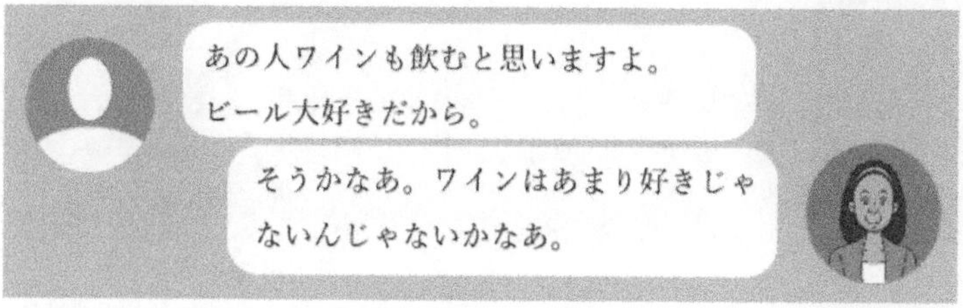
あの人ワインも飲むと思いますよ。ビール大好きだから。
そうかなあ。ワインはあまり好きじゃないんじゃないかなあ。

☐ certain
☐ tentative
☒ skeptical

Ex. 3.

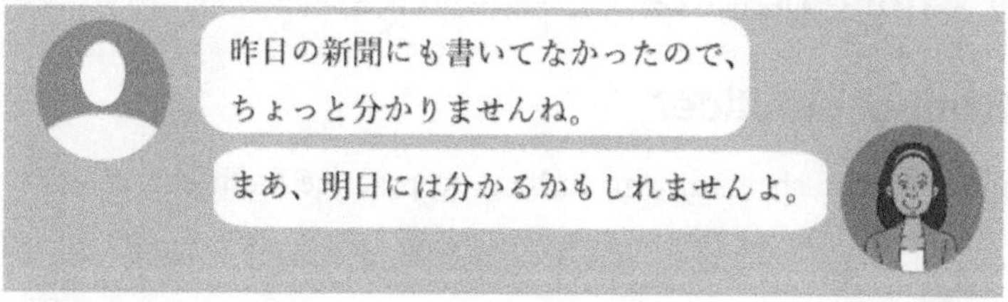
昨日の新聞にも書いてなかったので、ちょっと分かりませんね。
まあ、明日には分かるかもしれませんよ。

☐ certain
☒ tentative
☐ skeptical

4.

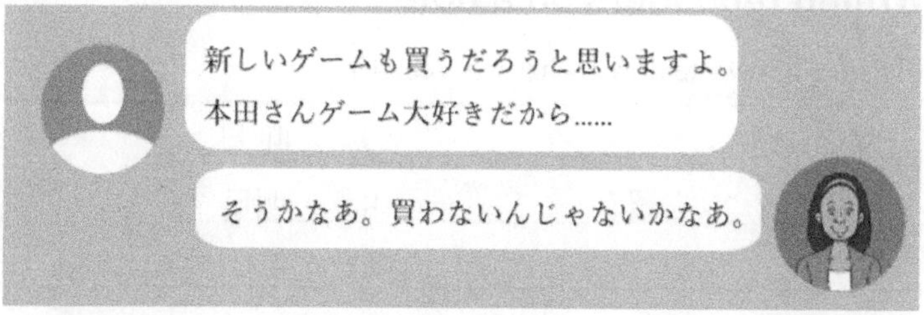
新しいゲームも買うだろうと思いますよ。本田さんゲーム大好きだから......
そうかなあ。買わないんじゃないかなあ。

☐ certain
☐ tentative
☐ skeptical

5.

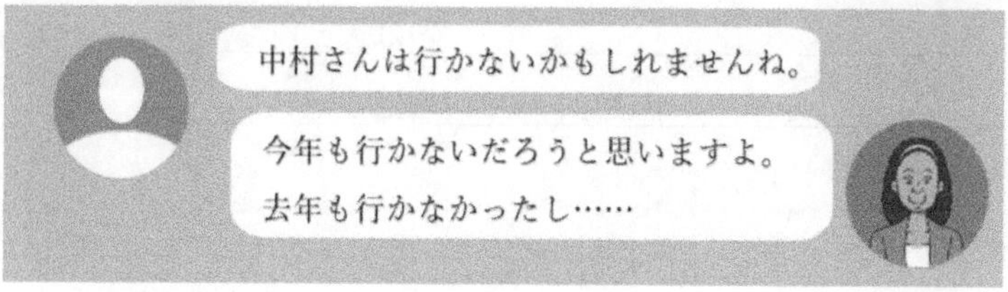
中村さんは行かないかもしれませんね。
今年も行かないだろうと思いますよ。去年も行かなかったし……

☐ certain
☐ tentative
☐ skeptical

6.

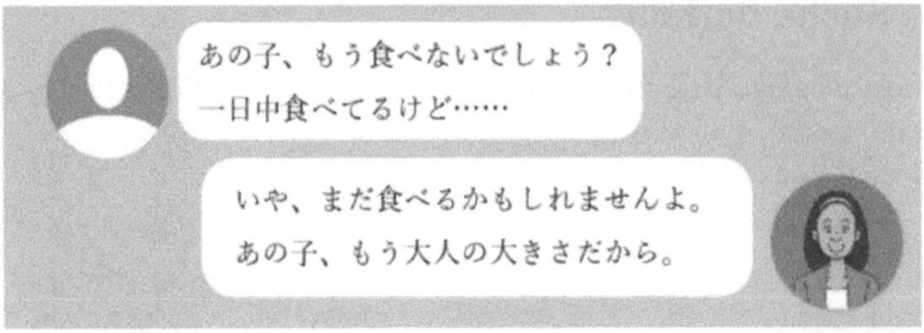
あの子、もう食べないでしょう？
一日中食べてるけど……
いや、まだ食べるかもしれませんよ。
あの子、もう大人の大きさだから。

☐ certain

☐ tentative

☐ skeptical

7.

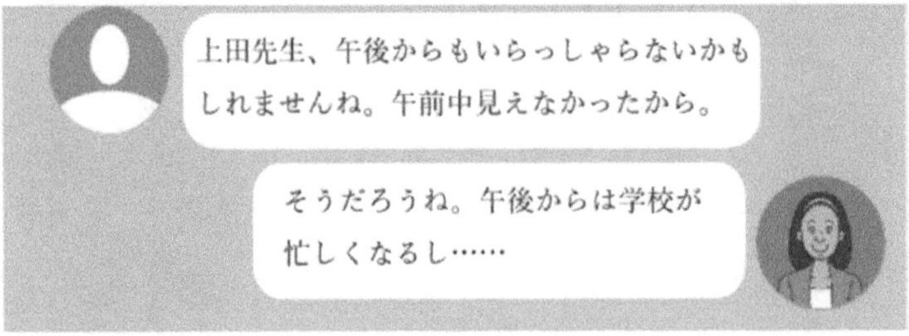
上田先生、午後からもいらっしゃらないかもしれませんね。午前中見えなかったから。
そうだろうね。午後からは学校が忙しくなるし……

☐ certain

☐ tentative

☐ skeptical

書き練習 Writing practice

文字練習 Symbol practice

Use the Symbol Practice sheets in Appendix A to practice kanji characters # 68-78 for Scene 10-8.

10-8-3W Writing reminders on a note

Listen to the dialogue and write down what was recalled.

Ex. 1. ピザを食べた のは 昨日

Ex. 2. 新しいパソコンを買う のは 明日

3. __________ のは ______

4. __________ のは ______

5. __________ のは ______

6. __________ のは ______

◆ Scene 10-9 練習 Practice

読み練習 Reading practice

10-9-1R Expectation vs. reality

Read the following statements and identify what is being discussed and how it compares to what was expected.

Ex. 1.	思ったより大きいですね、この会社。	Company is bigger than expected.
Ex. 2.	外国の人は去年ほど来ませんでしたね。	Not as many foreigners came as last year.
3.	仕事で来てる人が少ないですね、思ったより。	____________________
4.	今年は思ったほど国外に行く人が多くないですね。	____________________
5.	今年の日本語学生会は去年去年のよりよりいいですね。	____________________
6.	それほど新しくないですね、会田さんのスマホ。	____________________
7.	社会学のほうがビジネスよりも好きですね、思ったより。	____________________
8.	大学生はそれほど忙しくないでしょう。	____________________

10-9-2R Receiving words of advice

Read the following words of advice and identify whether it is likely given in a college (大学) or work setting (会社).

Ex. 1.	この仕事はそうじゃなくて、こうするんですよ。	☐ 大学	☒ 会社
Ex. 2.	日本語学生会のことはなんでも聞いてね。分からないことが多いかもしれないけど。	☒ 大学	☐ 会社
3.	がっかりしないでね。でも日本の会社ではそうはしないんだよ。	☐ 大学	☐ 会社

4. 行ってみたい会社にメールすることだけど、ちょっと先生に聞きに行ってみようよ。 □ 大学 □ 会社

5. オフィスにいない時はあまり仕事しないことだね。 □ 大学 □ 会社

6. 外国人が多くなってきている社会の中で、英語が分からなくて仕事をやめる人は少なくないので、大学にいる時にビジネス英語も少しはやっておいてくださいね。 □ 大学 □ 会社

7. ペーパー書くとかクラス行くとかで忙しいと思うけど、大学の後のことも今からプランしておこう！ □ 大学 □ 会社

書き練習 Writing practice

文字練習 Symbol practice

Use the Symbol Practice sheets in Appendix A to practice kanji characters # 79–83 for Scene 10-9.

10-9-3W Jotting down a schedule

A new member of your dorm is Japanese and is telling you his schedule. Write it down on the calendar below.

	午前中	午後
月	Ex. 1. 大学	
火	大学	
水	大学	
木		
金	Ex. 2. ネットワークビジネス会社	
土		
日		

◆ 評価 Assessment

Answer sheet templates are provided in Appendix B for the Assessment sections.

聞いてみよう Listening comprehension

Read the context, listen to the audio, and then answer the questions based on what you hear. If you hear something unfamiliar, focus on what you know to determine the correct answer.

1. Brian and Kawamura-san are talking after a baseball game that they went to watch together.
   a. What was disappointing about the baseball game?
   b. What made them feel nervous?
2. You overheard this exchange at a restaurant.
   a. What is the relationship between the man and the woman?
   b. What is the man's initial question?
   c. How does the woman respond to this question?
   d. How many people are in the woman's party?
   e. What recommendation does the man make? Why does he make this recommendation?
3. You overheard this exchange between a customer and a waiter at the next table at a restaurant.
   a. What does the woman order? Be specific.
4. Sasha went to a new restaurant with her roommate, Eri, who is trying a new dessert.
   a. What does Eri think of the dessert? Why does she think this?
   b. How does Sasha describe the dessert?
5. Kanda-san approaches Section Chief Yagi to ask a question.
   a. Why does Kanda-san apologize?
   b. What information is Kanda-san confirming?
   c. What reason does Kanda-san give for confirming this information?
   d. What does Section Chief Yagi ultimately request of Kanda-san?
6. Kanda-san introduces Smith-san, who is new to the office.
   a. For what purpose has Smith-san come to the office?
   b. What was Kanda-san's mistake? What correction did Smith-san offer?
   c. What reason does Kanda-san give for making the mistake?
   d. Based on Smith-san's explanation, why would this be an easy mistake to make?

7. Smith-san gives her self-introduction, following a brief introduction by Kanda-san.

   a. What is Smith-san's full name?
   b. What explanation does she give for her name?
   c. What does she say regarding her Japanese ability?
   d. What is her career aspiration?
   e. What is she not very good at?
   f. How long will she be in the office?

8. Brian is looking through various college catalogs at the International Student Office and asks a staff member about one of them.

   a. What is Brian's initial question?
   b. How does the staff member respond?
   c. Regarding the university in question, list all the positive qualities that the staff member mentions.

9. Mrs. Shirai seems tense as she asks Ichiro about a recent exam he took.

   a. What subject was the exam on?
   b. How did Ichiro do?
   c. What reason does Mrs. Shirai offer for Ichiro's performance?
   d. Why does Ichiro think Mrs. Shirai is incorrect in her assessment?
   e. What two points does Mrs. Shirai make in response to Ichiro?
   f. Why does Ichiro feel there's nothing to be done about it?
   g. Why does Mrs. Shirai encourage Ichiro to work hard?

10. Sasha notices that division chief Yagi is not at her desk and asks Kanda-san about it.

   a. Why is Yagi-bucho not at her desk?
   b. Why is Sasha surprised?
   c. What two locations will Yagi-bucho visit?
   d. How long will Yagi-bucho be gone?

11. Ichiro is talking with his mother over breakfast.

   a. What is the topic of conversation?
   b. What was Brian doing?
   c. What is Ichiro's assessment of Brian's actual ability?

使ってみよう Dry run

For each of the following, listen to the audio and respond to what was said based on the context.

1. When an older member of your group asks about another member, Sato-san, give him your conjecture that it might be that she (a) already went home; (b) is

dreaming; (c) gave up; (d) isn't good at it; (e) is feeling nervous; and (f) didn't have time to prepare.

2. Another member of your group, someone who is fairly close to you, asks about you. Give him as a reason for your action or current status some background information as follows: (a) you already saw it once; (b) you have meetings all day long; (c) you don't care for Chinese food (lit. Chinese food is your weakness); (d) it wasn't as difficult as you'd thought; (e) you didn't know how to reserve them; (f) you more or less practiced in advance; and (g) you were in the middle of class.
3. You are speaking with Nagano-san, your supervisor. When asked about a new restaurant, tell her that you went there last week. You had a lunch combination, but it was really salty. Moreover, it took more than 40 minutes for dessert to come out. Conclude your remark by stating that you can't recommend it. It's better to eat at the company cafeteria.
4. You are at a restaurant. Go through the routine by (a) telling the host that you don't have a reservation and asking if they have seats available; (b) telling the waiter that there are 4 people in your party; (c) telling the waiter that you don't mind waiting (for the seats); (d) telling the waiter that you'd like a little time, and you'd like beer to start with; (e) ordering two orders of the tempura combo and two orders of the BBQ meat combo; and (f) telling the waiter that for the BBQ meat combo, you don't want a lot of rice.
5. You are talking to a friend about a textbook. When your friend doesn't know which textbook you're talking about, tell him that it's the textbook that the student who's always studying in the Exchange Student Center was reading.
6. When a friend of yours tells you she doesn't want to go to Europe anymore, ask for clarification by pointing out that she had said something like she wanted to go (there).
7. When a friend says something you think might be implying something negative, ask what he means (lit. what kind of thing).

Now it's your turn to start the conversation based on the given context. Listen to how the other person reacts to you. For some items, you may not get a verbal response. Don't be concerned if you hear things you have not yet learned.

8. You are speaking to your Japanese language partner during a one-month stay in Japan. Tell her your intention to do the following during (by the end of) this month, in preparation of your return: (a) go see a noh performance; (b) conduct some experiment; (c) write an academic article; (d) get used to driving on a Japanese road; (e) look into things about Japanese graduate schools; (f) learn how to make Japanese cuisine; and (g) take the exam at the Japanese language center one more time.
9. You are speaking to a friend. Find out if he likes (a) vegetables; (b) fruit; (c) noodles; (d) French cuisine; (e) beer; (f) cola; (g) dessert; (h) spicy things; and (i) BBQ meat.
10. You are talking to a *senpai*, who is proficient in a number of languages. Admire the fact that she is strong (proficient) in foreign languages.
11. You found a bag that has apparently been forgotten. Ask a co-worker if he knows the name of the student that was carrying this brown bag.

12. You have just arrived to a work meeting late. Go through an apology to your superior by (a) apologizing for being late; (b) stating that it was your fault (lit. you were the one who was bad); (c) after being asked a second time what happened, explaining that the bus was late; (d) stating that you will certainly come by 10 minutes before (the meeting starts) from now on; (e) closing with another apology.
13. You have just found out that someone said the cake you made didn't taste very good. Ask a group of friends who it was that said that the cake you made was bad.
14. A friend of yours has just said that he is going to do a certain task by himself. Suggest that rather than doing it by himself, it would be better if everyone did it.
15. You have encountered a situation and are unsure how to proceed. Ask a *senpai* what to do in this kind of situation (lit. at this kind of time).
16. You are speaking to a friend. You are at a restaurant and notice someone who looks familiar. Ask your friend if the person playing the piano over there isn't Yamashita-san.

読んでみよう Contextualized reading

(1) You received the following memo attached to a box of cookies. Read the memo and answer the questions that follow.

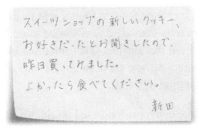

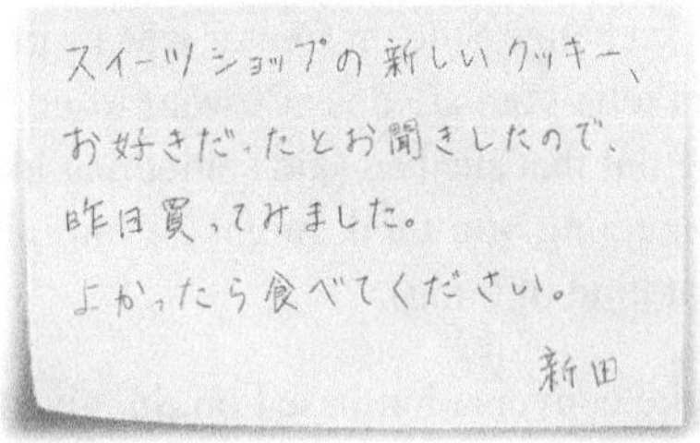
スイーツショップの新しいクッキー、
お好きだったとお聞きしたので、
昨日買ってみました。
よかったら食べてください。
新田

a. Who wrote the memo?
b. How are the cookies described?
c. When were they purchased. Why?

(2) Read the following memo attached to a document and answer the questions that follow.

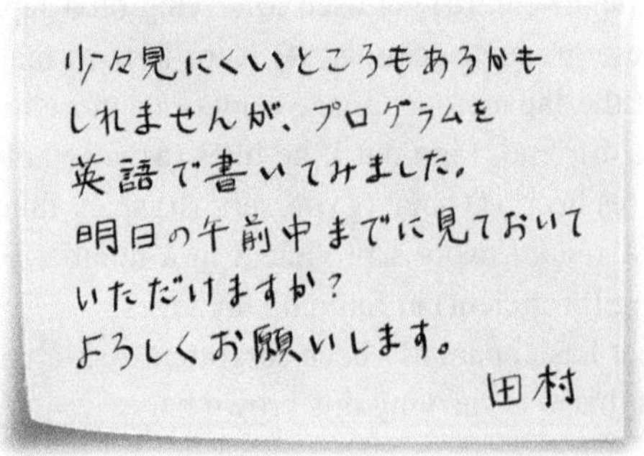
少々見にくいところもあるかも
しれませんが、プログラムを
英語で書いてみました。
明日の午前中までに見ておいて
いただけますか？
よろしくお願いします。
田村

a. Who wrote the memo?
b. What did the writer attempt to do? What is the possible problem that the writer addresses?
c. What request does the writer make? When is the deadline?

(3) Read the following chat between Eiichi and Kanda-san and answer the questions that follow.

a. What question does Eiichi ask first? How does Kanda-san respond?
b. What are they going to do? When? Where?
c. What is Eiichi going to do in preparation for their activity?
d. What additional suggestion does Kanda-san make? Why?
e. Where is Kanda-san going to meet Eiichi?

書き取り Dictation

Listen, imagine the context, repeat silently what you hear, then write it down.

1. ____。
2. ____。
3. ____。
4. ____。
5. ____。
6. ____。
7. ____。
8. ____。

書いてみよう Contextualized writing

1. Invite your friends for drinks after work on a sticky note.

2. You baked something for Nakata-san who bought you some cookies yesterday. On a memo attached to the container, (a) thank Nakata-san for buying and bringing you cookies yesterday, and (b) tell her to try what you baked with an explanation that it might be a little difficult to chew (lit. eat), but it turned out better than you expected.

3. You wrote a handout for your presentation in Japanese. Ask your colleague, Tamura-san, if he could look it over. In your memo, (a) explain that you attempted to write the handout in Japanese because you are thinking of doing a presentation at work in Japanese; and (b) ask him if he could look it over by tomorrow afternoon (don't forget to acknowledge his busy schedule!).

知ってる? What do you know?

Select the most appropriate option and write the letter on your answer sheet.

1. You offer to open all the windows so that the room will be cooler when guests arrive later on.

   窓(まど)を開(あ)けて______________か。(BTS 1)

   a. しましょう

   b. おきましょう

   c. きましょう

2. You offer to go and buy some sweets (and then return).

   お菓子(かし)を買(か)って_________か。(BTS 1)

   a. きましょう

   b. おきましょう

   c. いきましょう

3. You tell your friend that you've been thinking about quitting your job.

   仕事(しごと)____________と思(おも)っているけど……。(BTS 2)

   a. 辞(や)める

   b. 辞(や)めましょう

   c. 辞(や)めよう

4. You tried to send the email to your supervisor, but (you couldn't).
あのメール________けど……。(BTS 2)

a. お送(おく)りした
b. 送(おく)ってみよう
c. 送(おく)ろうとした

5. 勉強中(べんきょうちゅう)________、お邪魔(じゃま)したくないんです。(BTS 3)

a. から
b. ので
c. なので

6. まだできていない__________、もう少(すこ)し待(ま)ってください。(BTS 3)

a. ので
b. なので
c. だから

7. When we add ～中(じゅう)に to a time word, the pattern means _______ the time span. (BTS 4)

a. by the end of
b. all throughout
c. sometime during

8. When we add ～中(ちゅう) to an activity word, the pattern means ________the activity. (BTS 4)

a. by the end of
b. in the midst of
c. sometime during

9. You apologize for being late for the meeting.
遅(おそ)く__________ すみませんでした。(BTS 5)

a. なったので
b. なって
c. なったから

10. You ask if Professor Kawamura is in.
川村先生(かわむらせんせい)____________________か。(BTS 6)

a. いらっしゃいます
b. でいらっしいます
c. でございます

11. You ask the professor if her husband is ill.
ご主人(しゅじん)、ご病気(びょうき)_______________________か。(BTS 6)

a. ございます

b. いらっしゃいます

c. でいらっしゃいます

12. You ask your teacher if she has the keys to the classroom.
先生(せんせい)、教室(きょうしつ)の鍵(かぎ)、お持(も)ち______________か。(BTS 6)

a. します

b. です

c. ございます

13. You tell your supervisor that you haven't heard the results of your application yet.
まだ何(なに)も伺(うかが)って____________________。(BTS 6)

a. おりません

b. しません

c. ございません

14. You've been asked about a dormitory on campus. You reply:
ちょっと不便(ふべん)________________かもしれない。(BTS 8)

a. だ

b. な

c. Ø

15. You've been asked about what they served last night at the party. You reply:
天(てん)ぷらかも____________。(BTS 8)

a. しらない

b. しれなかった

c. しれない

16. You tell your friend there's really no need to be troubled about the homework.
困(こま)る_______ないよ。(BTS 9)

a. の

b. こと

c. もの

17. You ask if your roommate did such things as make a reservation in preparation for your trip.
予約した________？(BTS 11)

a. かも
b. とか
c. のか

18. You've been asked which you like to do more, swim or jog. You reply:
泳ぐ________ジョッギングの方が好き。(BTS 12)

a. ほど
b. も
c. より

19. You've been asked whether it's more fun to do the project by yourself or with someone else. You reply:
一緒にする________一人でやるのはやっぱり面白くない 。(BTS 12)

a. ほど
b. より
c. ほう

20. The suffix 〜かた attaches to the ________ and the compound becomes ________. (BTS 13)

a. - 〜て form・an Adjective
b. Verb stem・a の Noun
c. Verb root・a な Noun

21. You describe how to use the new coffee maker to your roommate.
_______使うよ。(BTS 15)

a. こう
b. これ
c. こんな

22. Commas in Japanese ________. (BTL 1)

a. follow the same rules as English
b. are borrowed from Chinese
c. can be used wherever a speaker might take a breath

第 11 幕
Act 11

どうしたらいい？

What shall I do?

目は 口ほどに物を言う

Eyes say as much as words.

◆ Scene 11-1 練習 Practice

理解練習 Comprehension practice

11-1-1C Business phone conversations (BTS 2)

For each phone conversation, write the name of the person calling. Then select the purpose of the current phone call from the options provided. If the purpose is to confirm the time of an appointment or event, write the date and time.

	Name:	Purpose of the call:	Day and time of the appointment or event:
Ex. 1.	Takagi	c	not mentioned
2.			
3.			
4.			

a. To express gratitude
b. To confirm the time of an appointment or event
c. To speak to a person in the operations division

実演練習 Performance practice

11-1-2P Agreeing conditionally (BTS 1)

When Sato-san, a fellow team member, proposes an action, agree with her, given the condition she also suggests.

Ex. 1.

Sato-san	新しく買いませんか。必要だと思いますが. . . . . .。	Shouldn't we buy a new one? I think we need it.
You	そうですね。必要だったら新しく買いましょう。	Yes, if it's necessary, let's buy a new one.

Ex. 2.

Sato-san	この問題は山田さんに任せませんか。よく知っていると思いますが ……。	Shouldn't we leave this issue up to Yamada-san? I think he is knowledgeable about it.
You	そうですね。よく知っているんだったら山田さんに任せましょう。	Yes, if he is knowledgeable about it, let's leave it up to Yamada-san.

11-1-3P Responding affirmatively with elaboration (BTS 1)

When Tomoda-san, a junior work colleague, asks if you will do something, respond affirmatively and provide some additional information about the conditions under which you will do it, based on the prompt.

Ex. 1.

Tomoda-san	富士山を登るんですか。	Are you going to climb Mt. Fuji?
You	はい、天気がよかったら富士山を登ります。	Yes, if the weather is good I'll climb Mt. Fuji.

Ex. 2.

Tomoda-san	お茶淹れるんですか。	Are we going to put on tea?
You	はい、美馬さんが来たらお茶淹れます。	Yes, when Mima-san gets here we'll put on tea.

Ex. 1. If the weather is good
Ex. 2. When Mima-san gets here
3. When the weather clears up
4. When these run out
5. If Murata-san doesn't know
6. If it's not big
7. If I have time
8. When I finish this job
9. If there aren't any trains

11-1-4P Offering to switch (BTS 3)

When a client on the phone mentions who he thinks the appropriate person in your group is, tell him that you will get (literally, switch with) that person.

Ex. 1.

Sato-san	部長さんがよくご存知なんですが、今いらっしゃいますか？	Your division chief knows this well, but is she there?
You	はい、部長と代わりますので、少々お待ちください。	Yes, I'll get the division chief, so please wait a moment.

Ex. 2.

Sato-san	加藤さんがご専門なんですが、今お時間おありですか？	Kato-san is the specialist, but does he have time now?
You	はい、加藤と代わりますので、少々お待ちください。	Yes, I'll get Kato, so please wait a moment.

◆ Scene 11-2 練習 Practice

理解練習 Comprehension practice

11-2-1C Meanings of ～たら +non-past (BTS 1, 5)

Mark the function of each utterance by selecting (a) statement, (b) request, or (c) suggestion (either giving or seeking a suggestion).

Ex. 1.	☐ Statement	☒ Request	☐ Suggestion
Ex. 2.	☐ Statement	☐ Request	☒ Suggestion
3.	☐ Statement	☐ Request	☐ Suggestion
4.	☐ Statement	☐ Request	☐ Suggestion
5.	☐ Statement	☐ Request	☐ Suggestion
6.	☐ Statement	☐ Request	☐ Suggestion
7.	☐ Statement	☐ Request	☐ Suggestion
8.	☐ Statement	☐ Request	☐ Suggestion
9.	☐ Statement	☐ Request	☐ Suggestion

実演練習 Performance practice

11-2-2P Suggesting that it's excessive (BTS 6)

You and your friend, Yoshida-san, are talking about a mutual acquaintance, Saito-kun. Listen to Yoshida-san's observation and make an evaluation, assuming agreement from your friend, that Saito-kun tends to be excessive in whatever he does.

Ex. 1.

Yoshida-san	斎藤君ね、この間お客さんが持ってきたお土産のクッキーね、全部食べちゃったんですよ。	Saito-kun, you know, he ate all of the cookies that the visitor brought as a souvenir!
You	へえ。ちょっと食べ過ぎですよね。	Wow! That's eating too much, isn't it!

Ex. 2.

Yoshida-san	斎藤君は先週もね、ずっと勉強して３日ぐらい寝なかったんですよ。	Saito-kun, last week, too, you know, he studied the whole time and didn't sleep for as long as three days!
You	へえ。ちょっと勉強のし過ぎですよね。	Wow! That's studying too much, isn't it!

11-2-3P Asking what to do (BTS 5)

Yagi-bucho has been talking to one of your co-workers about doing something. When Yagi-bucho tells you to do it too, ask her for clarification based on the prompt. She will address you as Wang-san.

Ex. 1.

Yagi-bucho	ワンさんも作ってください。	Wang-san, you make some too.
You	はい。あのう、何枚作ったらいいでしょうか。	Okay. Um, how many should I make?

Ex. 2.

Yagi-bucho	ワンさんも行ってください。	Wang-san, you go too.
You	はい。あのう、どこに行ったらいいでしょうか。	Okay. Um, where should I go?

Ex. 1. How many (pamphlets)?
Ex. 2. Where?
3. Where?
4. Which one (of five)?
5. What time?
6. When?
7. Who?
8. Which one (of two)?
9. How many (pictures)?

11-2 腕試し Tryout

Ask for someone's advice on something you have a question about.

◆ Scene 11-3 練習 Practice

理解練習 Comprehension practice

11-3-1C Meanings of ～ことにする (BTS 7)

Mark the function of ことにする in each utterance by selecting (a) decision, (b) routine (i.e., routine action), or (c) assumption.

Ex. 1.	☒ Decision	☐ Routine	☐ Assumption
Ex. 2.	☐ Decision	☒ Routine	☐ Assumption
3.	☐ Decision	☐ Routine	☐ Assumption
4.	☐ Decision	☐ Routine	☐ Assumption
5.	☐ Decision	☐ Routine	☐ Assumption
6.	☐ Decision	☐ Routine	☐ Assumption
7.	☐ Decision	☐ Routine	☐ Assumption
8.	☐ Decision	☐ Routine	☐ Assumption
9.	☐ Decision	☐ Routine	☐ Assumption

11-3-2C Who are these people?

Listen to the conversations and write the name of the person under each illustration.

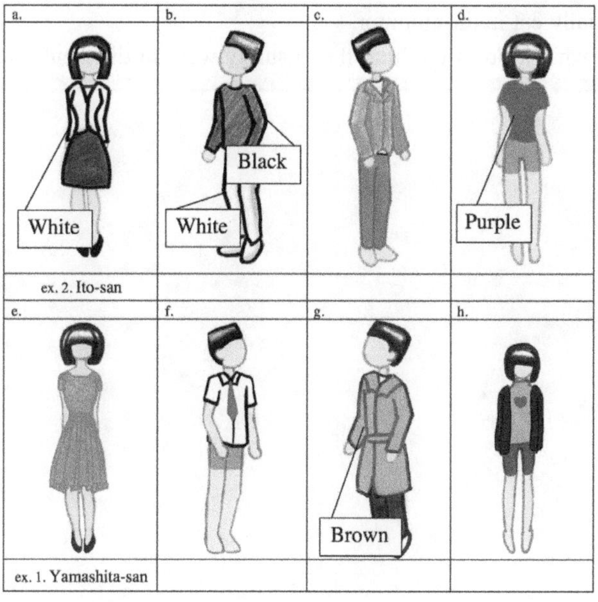

実演練習 Performance practice

11-3-3P Agreeing with a critical opinion and suggesting it's excessive (BTS 6)

Respond to your group member Taguchi-san's comments about a recent event/encounter, suggesting that what the two of you experienced could be deemed excessive.

Ex. 1.

Taguchi-san	よく遊びましたねえ、この間。	We played hard the other day, didn't we!
You	全く。あんなに遊んだら遊び過ぎですよね。	Indeed. Playing that much is a bit much, isn't it.

Ex. 2.

Taguchi-san	かなり濃かったですねえ、あのスープ。	It was rather strong, that soup, no?
You	全く。あんなに濃かったら濃過ぎですよね。	Indeed. That level of flavor is a bit much, isn't it.

11-3 腕試し Tryout

1. Ask someone what the seasons are like in the place they are from. For example, you could ask how cold it gets in the winter, when spring usually begins, or what kind of foods they usually eat in the summer.
2. Ask someone what kind of clothing they usually wear in different seasons in the place they are from.

◆ Scene 11-4　練習 Practice

理解練習 Comprehension practice

11-4-1C Who is it? (BTS 11)

Write the family term mentioned in the space provided, based on the options below.

Ex. 1. Wife (polite)

Ex. 2. Girlfriend

3. ______________________

4. ______________________

5. ______________________

6. ______________________

7. ______________________

8. ______________________

9. ______________________

Grandmother (in-group)	Grandfather (in-group)	Girlfriend
Grandmother (polite)	Grandfather (polite)	Boyfriend
Uncle (in-group)	Aunt (in-group)	Cousin (in-group)
Uncle (polite)	Aunt (polite)	Cousin (polite)
Wife (in-group)	Wife (polite)	
Husband (in-group)	Husband (polite)	

11-4-2C From a literary perspective . . . (BTS 10)

Write an English equivalent of the term mentioned that uses ～的 in the space provided.

Ex. 1. Literary ____________________

Ex. 2. Positive ____________________

3. ____________________

4. ____________________

5. ____________________

6. ____________________

7. ____________________

8. ____________________

実演練習 Performance practice

11-4-3P Inquiring about relatives (BTS 11)

Based on the numbers on the family diagram of Ikegami-san, your new friend, ask politely about her relatives. Remember to use 方, a polite alternative to 人, in your questions.

Ex. 1.

You	あの、ご主人様ってどんな方 ですか?	So, what's your husband like?
Ikegami-san	真面目だけど、結構面白い人ですよ。	He's serious, but pretty funny.

Ex. 2.

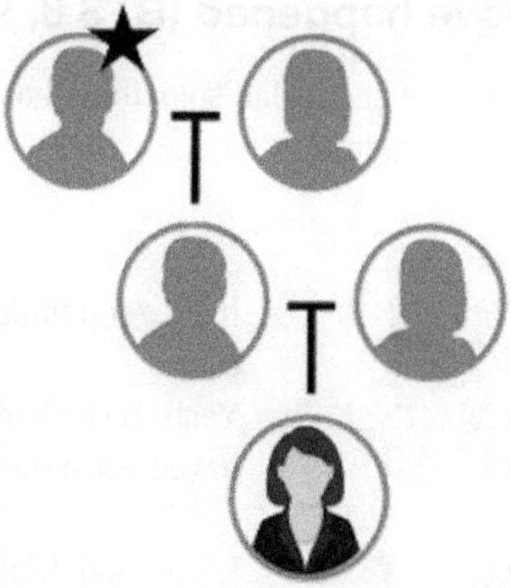

You	あの、おじい様ってどんな方ですか？	So, what's your grandfather like?
Ikegami-san	ちょっと変わった人ですね。何考えてるかよくわからない。ま、悪い人ではないですけどね。	He's a little weird. I never really know what he's thinking. But he's not a bad person, though.

3.

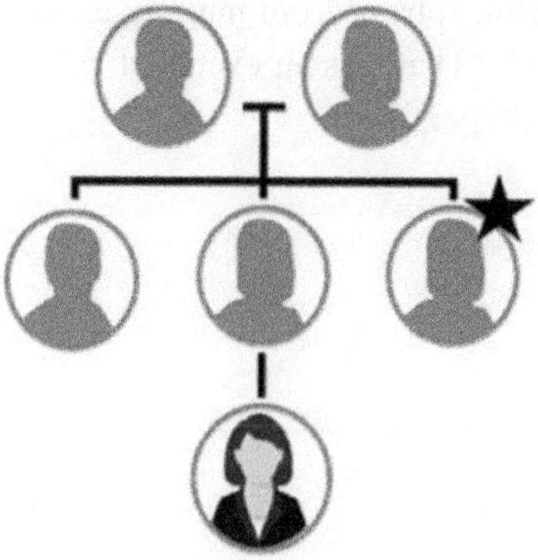

4.

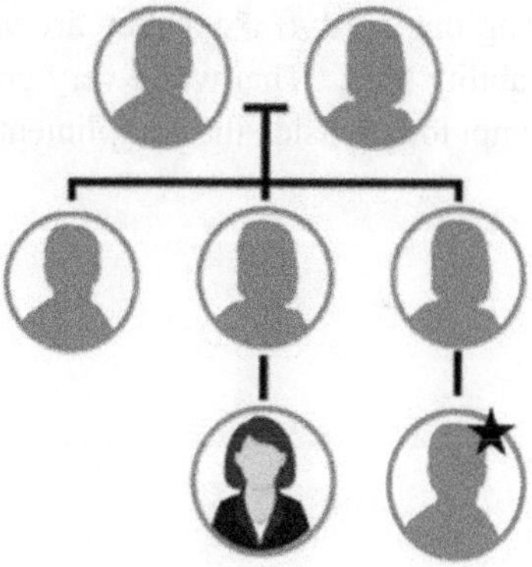

5.

6.

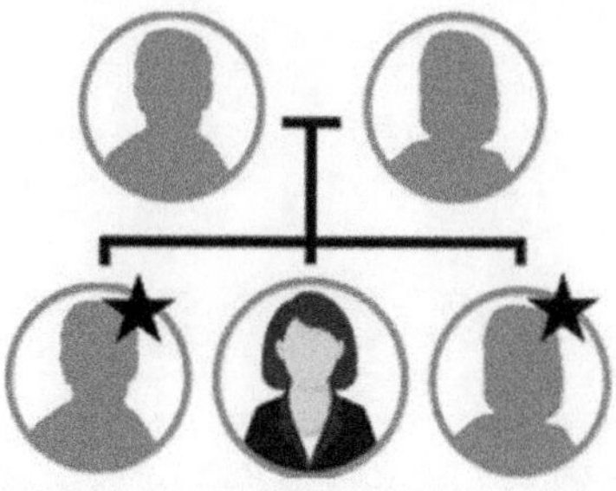

11-4-4P Saying what would have happened (BTS 8, 9)

When Yoshida-san, a co-worker, comments that she's glad something happened, reply that it could have been a big problem if it hadn't happened.

Ex. 1.

Yoshida-san	山田さんが来てよかったですね!	It's a good thing Yamada-san came!
You	ええ。来ていなかったら大変なことになっていたかもしれませんね。	Yeah. If she hadn't come it could have been a disaster.

Ex. 2.

Yoshida-san	諦めなくてよかったですね!	It's a good thing we didn't give up!
You	ええ。諦めていたら大変なことになっていたかもしれませんね。	Yeah. If we had given up it could have been a disaster.

11-4 腕試し Tryout

Pay someone a compliment. If you are complimenting one of their possessions, refrain from using the word 好き. If they are your superior, refrain from making an evaluation of their ability (e.g., "That was a very good lesson," "That was an excellent talk," etc.). If they attempt to turn aside the compliment, be politely persistent.

◆ Scene 11-5　練習 Practice

理解練習 Comprehension practice

11-5-1C Where does it hurt? (BTS 14)

Match the body part with the type of pain or other affliction the man describes.

Throbbing

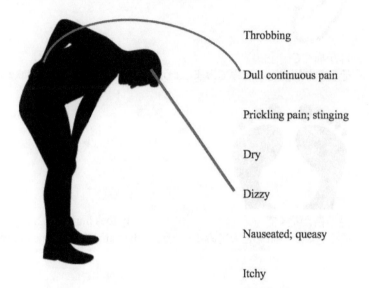

Dull continuous pain

Prickling pain; stinging

Dry

Dizzy

Nauseated; queasy

Itchy

11-5-2C Meanings of ～たら +past (BTS 9, 12)

Mark the function of each utterance by selecting (a) imagined (i.e., an imagined situation that never actually happened), or (b) uncontrollable (i.e., something that actually happened but the result of what the speaker did was unexpected or outside his or her control).

Ex. 1.	☒ Imagined	☐ Uncontrollable
Ex. 2.	☐ Imagined	☒ Uncontrollable
3.	☐ Imagined	☐ Uncontrollable
4.	☐ Imagined	☐ Uncontrollable
5.	☐ Imagined	☐ Uncontrollable
6.	☐ Imagined	☐ Uncontrollable
7.	☐ Imagined	☐ Uncontrollable
8.	☐ Imagined	☐ Uncontrollable
9.	☐ Imagined	☐ Uncontrollable
10.	☐ Imagined	☐ Uncontrollable

実演練習 Performance practice

11-5-3P Indicating where there is pain

You are seeing a doctor. Indicate where you have pain, according to the illustration.

Ex. 1.

You	耳が痛くて……。	My ear hurts, and . . .
Doctor	そうですか。ちょっとみてみましょう。	Is that right? Let me take a look.

Ex. 2.

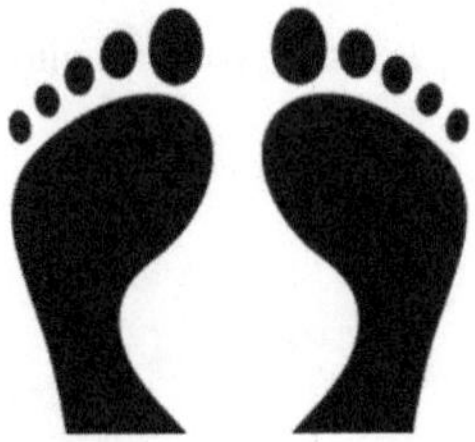

You	足の指が痛くて……。	My toes hurt, and . . .
Doctor	そうですか。ちょっとみてみましょう。	Is that right? Let me take a look.

3.

4.

5.

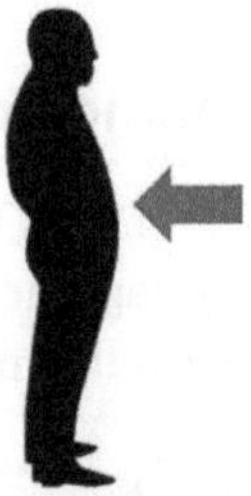

6.

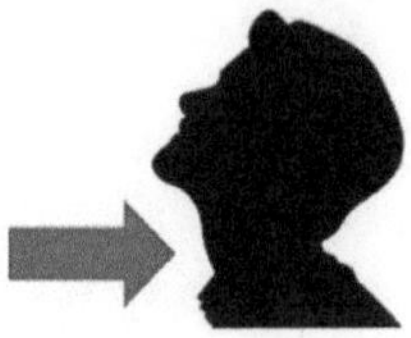

7.

8.

11-5-4P It wasn't what I expected (BTS 12)

When your friend Yuya checks on what you thought about something, agree, but also clarify that when you tried it, it wasn't as you thought it would be.

Ex. 1.

Yuya-kun	難しそうだったでしょう?	Didn't it seem difficult to you?
You	うん。でもやってみたらそんなに難しくなかったよ。	Yeah, but when I tried doing it, it wasn't that difficult.

Ex. 2.

Yuya-kun	楽しそうだったでしょう?	Didn't it seem fun to you?
You	うん。でもやってみたらそんなに楽しくなかったよ。	Yeah, but when I tried doing it, it wasn't that fun.

11-5 腕試し Tryout

Tell someone about a time that you got sick. Mention how you felt, and anything you did to try and get better.

◆ Scene 11-6 練習 Practice

実演練習 Performance practice

11-6-1P Echoing the key idea (BTS 15)

One of the strategies of being an engaged listener is to echo part of the storyteller's statement. Practice echoing the punchline, usually indicated by a slightly raised voice, as you listen to a group member tell a story.

Ex. 1.

Taguchi-san	先週の火曜日だったかな、朝起きたらすっごい雪で。	Was it Tuesday last week? When we got up in the morning, there was a huge amount of snow.
You	雪!	Snow!

Ex. 2.

Taguchi -san	母はね、積極的な人で、やると決めたらもうすぐ、その日、じゃなくその時に始めちゃうんですよ。	My mother, you know, being a pro-active person, once she determines that she is going to do something, she starts not on that day, but at that moment.
You	その時に。	At that moment.

11-6-2P Asking topic-determining questions (BTS 15)

Another important role of an engaged listener is to determine the course of the conversation. Practice asking a question to steer the direction of the story as you listen to a group member tell a story. Listen to the sample prompting questions provided on the audio as the story goes on. The listener acknowledges the end of the story (#7) with そうですか.

Ex. 1.

Taguchi-san	この間ね、新しくジャケットを買ったんですよ。	The other day, I bought a new jacket, you know.
You	へえ、どんなジャケットですか?	Wow, what kind of jacket?

Ex. 2.

Taguchi -san	デパート歩いて見てたら、ポケットがたくさん付いてるやつがあったんですよ。あ、これはなかなか実用的だと思ってね、買おうかと思って値段いくらか聞いて、もうびっくり。	I was walking and looking in a department store when I saw one with a lot of pockets. This was quite practical, I thought, so thinking that I might buy it, I asked how much it was, and I was astonished.
You	いくらでした？	How much was it?

理解実演練習 Comprehension and performance practice

11-6-3CP Being an engaged listener (BTS 15)

In audio 1, you will hear a conversation in which Misaki tells a story (something that happened that was embarrassing, scary, etc.) to an acquaintance at a casual gathering. Part of being an engaged listener is understanding what you are hearing. Listen to audio 1, and write a simple summary of the main points of the story you hear. You don't need to understand all the details. For example, if you hear a type of food mentioned and you don't know what it is, but you know the speaker is talking about food, you can just write "food."

After you've finished the summary, play the part of an engaged listener by using 相槌 as you listen to the story in audio 2, assuming that you are at the gathering with Misaki. Include 相槌 (not just sounds, but also head-nodding, etc.) that shows you have understood some of the content of the story.

After you have practiced being an engaged listener, listen to audio 1 again and compare what you did when listening to audio 2, which includes the listener's 相槌. Did you use a variety of different types of 相槌? How did the frequency of your 相槌 compare with the model?

Summary: ____

____

____

____

____

11-6 腕試し Tryout

1. Tell a story about something that happened to you that was embarrassing or otherwise noteworthy (e.g., surprising, funny, scary, etc.).
2. Listen to someone tell you a story. Show that you are listening through 相槌 expressions, as well as questions and comments related to the content of the story.

◆ Scene 11-7　練習 Practice

読み練習 Reading practice

11-7-1R Filling in if or when statements

Fill in the following statements into the sentences below. Each selection may be used once.

a. 読みにくかったら	d. 言ったら	g. インタビューのスーツだったら
b. お電話でしたら	e. 先生に聞いてみたら	h. 少なかったら
c. 疲れましたら	f. 作ったら	i. お子様でしたら

Ex. 1.　このケーキ、どうやって＿＿＿＿f＿＿＿＿いいんですか。

Ex. 2.　言語学の本、＿＿＿＿a＿＿＿＿すみません。

3.　＿＿＿＿＿＿＿＿＿＿よく水を飲んでくださいね。

4.　読んでも分からないんだったら＿＿＿＿＿＿＿＿＿＿いいと思うよ。

5.　あの話、中村さんになんて＿＿＿＿＿＿＿＿＿＿いいと思う?

6.　＿＿＿＿＿＿＿＿＿＿去年買っておいたよ。

7.　＿＿＿＿＿＿＿＿＿＿あちらにいらっしゃいましたよ。

8.　外国人が＿＿＿＿＿＿＿＿＿＿英語で話さなくてもいいですよ。

9.　＿＿＿＿＿＿＿＿＿＿あちらのをお使いください。

11-7-2R Giving suggestions

Choose the most appropriate suggestion from the options below. Each option may be used once.

a. してみたら	d. 電話してみたら	g. 世話してみたら
b. 待ったら	e. 読んでみたら	h. 行ってみたら
c. 話してみたら	f. 作ったら	i. 買ってみたら

Ex. 1. 英語で______c______?

Ex. 2. あのハムスター______g______?

3. このワイシャツ______________?

4. 言語学に______________?

5. キッチンで______________?

6. マニュアルきちんと______________?

7. 大学に______________?

8. バス、あと5分______________?

9. メールじゃなくて______________?

書き練習 Writing practice

文字練習 Symbol practice

Use the Symbol Practice sheets in Appendix A to practice kanji characters #84-92 for Scene 11-7.

11-7-3W Writing initial greetings in a letter

Complete the initial greetings of a letter by filling in the blanks. Use the verb or noun specified in parentheses.

Ex. 1.	いつもブログを<u>読んでくださって</u>ありがとうございます。	(reading)
Ex. 2.	先日は<u>お世話</u>になりました。	(care)
3.	先日は時間を____________________ありがとうございました。	(making)
4.	いつも________になっています。	(care)
5.	先日は__________でした。	(good work)
6.	先日は________ありがとうございました。	(phone call)
7.	いつもイラストを__________________ありがとうございます。	(using)

◆ Scene 11-8　練習 Practice

読み練習 Reading practice

11-8-1R Making logical decisions

Identify what decisions are made and write down the reason for each decision.

Ex. 1.　東大ほど高くないので、京大に行くことにしました。
Ex. 2.　車で行ったら時間がかかるから、電車で行こうと思ってるんだけど……。
3.　高いし、忙しくなるから、カンファレンスには出ないことにしている。
4.　東京には行かないことにしているんだ。人が多いし、お金もかかるし……。
5.　入りたくてもなかなかむずかしいところに入ったんだから、やっぱり京都大学に行くよ。
6.　外出中だったので、また後ほど来ることにしました。
7.　京都までの電車がもう出ていないので、タクシーを使うことにしました。

	Decision	Reason
Ex. 1.	Go to Kyoto University	not as expensive as Tokyo University
Ex. 2.	Go by train	it takes time if we go by car
3.	______	______
4.	______	______
5.	______	______
6.	______	______
7.	______	______

11-8-2R Expressing imagined conditions

Read the following statements and match them with the most logical imagined condition in the selections below.

a. おじさんの話を聞いていたら
b. 仕事のオファーがなかったら
c. 午前中にメールを出していたら
d. 大学からのメールを見ていなかったら
e.先月買っておいたら
f. カバンの中に入れておいたら
g. 東大を出ていたら

Ex. 1. ___a___、おばさんの話もすぐに分かったと思いますよ。
Ex. 2. ___e___、京都までのチケットはこんなに高くはならなかったでしょうね。
3. _______、今もっといい仕事をしていたと思います。
4. _______、女の子へのプレゼントもなくならなかったと思います。
5. _______、田口さんとは会ってなかったかもしれません。
6. _______、日本には行かなかったかもしれません。
7. _______、午後には話ができたと思いますよ。

書き練習 Writing practice

文字練習 Symbol practice

Use the Symbol Practice sheets in Appendix A to practice kanji characters #93-100 for Scene 11-8.

11-8-3W Writing down important information on a memo

Listen to the exchanges and write down the most important information specified in each.

Ex. 1. 駅前のコンビニ	Ex. 2. 電車
3.	4.
5.	6.
7.	8.

◆ Scene 11-9 練習 Practice

読み練習 Reading practice

11-9-1R Finishing a story with a punch line

Match the following stories with an appropriate punch line from the selections:

a. 私の左にもあったんですよ
b. 車のカギがなくなっていたんですよ
c. 先生のと同じ車だったんですよ
d. 中国語だったんですよ
e. 私が話している人が前を歩いていたんですよ
f. 仕事に行く時間になっていたんですよ

Ex. 1. 日本語で話してると思ったら、____d____!
Ex. 2. 電話で話していたら、____e____!
3. 遅くまで本を読んでいたら、________!
4. 早くアパートに帰ろうと思ったら、________!
5. 外にある車を見たら、________!
6. 右にもあると思ったら、________!

11-9-2R Telling a story

Put the following pieces of stories into a logical order.

Ex. 1.
a. 電話しようとしたら
b. かばんに入ってなくて
c. 電車が遅れてたから
d. まずいなって思ったんです。
c > a > b > d

Ex. 2.
a. 早く帰ろうと思って
b. もう9時になってて
c. びっくりしたよ
d. 大学を出たら
a > d > b > c

3.
a. びっくりしたよ
b. 私と同じ私立大学に行ってる人だと思って
c. まだ高校生だったから
d. 話してみたら
___ > ___ > ___ > ___

4.
a. 外をフラフラ歩いていたら
b. まずいなと思ったよ
c. 分からないところに出て
d. 何もすることないから
___ > ___ > ___ > ___

5.

a. 右から行こうとしたら
b. すごいスピードの車が来てね
c. 左がだめだったので
d. びっくりしたよ

___ > ___ > ___ > ___

6.

a. 駅から５分のところにあると思って
b. ５分じゃなくて１５分のところにあったから
c. かなり遅れたよ
d. 少し遅めに出たら

___ > ___ > ___ > ___

書き練習 Writing practice

文字練習 Symbol practice

Use the Symbol Practice sheets in Appendix A to practice kanji characters #101-108 for Scene 11-9.

11-9-3W Leaving a memo

Complete writing memos to your new roommate as prompted.

Ex. 1. will be late 月曜日は仕事でちょっと 遅くなります。 ________________	Ex. 2. okay to use my car 明日は 私の車使っていいですよ。 ________________	3. come home early 来週の水曜日はいつもより ________________。 ________________。
4. go by the same train 明日はいつもと ________________ ________________ どうですか？	5. on the left as you exit 車はアパートを ________________ ________________ にあります。	6. come home on foot 今日は車がないので ________________。 ________________。

◆ 評価 Assessment

Answer sheet templates are provided in Appendix B for the Assessment sections.

聞いてみよう Listening comprehension

Read the context, listen to the audio, and then answer the questions based on what you hear. If you hear something unfamiliar, rely on what you know to answer the question.

1. Mizuno-san at Ogaki-Shokai takes an in-coming phone call.
   a. What division does Mizuno-san work in?
   b. Who has called?
   c. When will their meeting take place? Be specific.
   d. Where will they meet?
2. Yamamura-san at another division takes a call from an internal line.
   a. What division does Yamamura-san work in?
   b. What month and date are mentioned? Why does Yamamura-san mention this date?
   c. What items does Yamamura-san need from the caller?
   d. Why does Yamamura-san mention the division chief?
3. Division Chief Yagi makes a phone call.
   a. Who is Yagi-bucho calling? What is this person's position?
   b. What apparently happened the other day?
   c. Regarding the main purpose of Yagi-bucho's call, what important information does she provide to the other person? Be specific.
4. Mizuno-san and a few others have gone out for a drink after work with Hayashi-san, a relatively new member.
   a. Why does Mizuno-san congratulate Hayashi-san?
   b. Why is Hayashi-san's *senpai* mentioned?
   c. When was this person Hayashi-san's *senpai*?
   d. How old is this person in relation to Hayashi-san?
   e. How does Hayashi-san explain their age?
5. A college professor congratulates one of his advisees.
   a. Why is the professor congratulating the advisee?
   b. What did the advisee decide? What other options were there?
   c. What reason does the advisee give for her decision?
   d. After hearing the reason, what compliment does the professor pay the advisee?

6. Two students are talking about an assignment in a foreign language.
   a. What does the male student ask?
   b. How does the female student respond?
   c. What will the male student probably do?
7. Kanda-san's office colleague Mizuno-san is pointing out an issue to him.
   a. What issue does Mizuno-san point out?
   b. What is Kanda-san's opinion? What reason does he give for his opinion?
   c. How does Mizuno-san respond to Kanda-san?
8. Kanda-san and his colleague are talking over drinks about bullying at elementary schools.
   a. What kind of issue does Kanda-san think it is?
   b. What has been happening for 10 years?
   c. What does Kanda-san wonder?
   d. What is Kanda-san's colleague's opinion?
   e. How does Kanda-san feel about this issue?
9. Mizuno-san seems upset with someone she supervises who has not been paying attention.
   a. How does the person respond to Mizuno-san's accusation?
   b. According to Mizuno-san, what has this person been doing while she has been speaking? What has the person not been doing?
   c. What comment does the person make about Mizuno-san?
   d. What does Mizuno-san ask the person? What is her reasoning for asking this question?
   e. Is the person able to answer Mizuno-san's question?
   f. What is Mizuno-san's request? What reason does she give for making this request?
10. Two new associates of Ogaki Shokai are talking over lunch.
    a. What is the topic of conversation?
    b. What does the woman say regarding this topic?
    c. What positive quality of the topic does the man mention?
11. Two college students are looking for a venue they can use for an event they are planning.
    a. What comment does the male student make about the venue?
    b. What comment does the female student make about the venue?
12. Eri remembers something that a fellow graduate student was talking about the other day and checks with him about it.
    a. What was going on the other day?
    b. How was it resolved?

13. Mizuno-san is concerned about an issue that Kanda-san resolves.

a. What is the issue?
b. Where did Mizuno-san think Yagi-san was?
c. What did Kanda-san do that resolved the issue? Why did Kanda-san decide to do this?

使ってみよう Dry run

For each of the following, listen to the audio and respond to what was said based on the context.

1. You are a representative of Ogaki Shokai, calling Aoi Shuppan to speak to Kimura-san in the Operations Division. When a representative of Aoi Shuppan answers the phone, appropriately convey your request.
2. Respond to a co-worker's inquiry by telling her that you decided to (a) not eat ice cream anymore; (b) get together Tuesday of next week; (c) wear a long sleeve shirt; (d) go to China and Korea next month; (e) wait for the time being.
3. When a *koohai* tells you that there's been no reply, suggest that for the time being you assume that it's okay and continue preparations.
4. A friend is curious about something. Tell her that (a) it's a present from your grandmother; (b) it's a photograph from a cousin; (c) it's an email to a professor; (d) it's homework that's due tomorrow.
5. When asked by a *koohai* what kind of person the intern Miura-san is, tell him that she's a little on the quiet side, but is very smart and works hard.
6. You are speaking to your host mother, who has noticed that something is wrong. Tell her that (a) when you woke up, your head was dizzy; (b) when you ate breakfast, you felt nauseated; (c) when you were eating ramen for lunch, your arm (started) stinging; (d) when you arrived home, your throat got dry and your head (started) throbbing.

For each of the following, say something that would be appropriate based on the description of the situation. Then compare what you said with the sample, and listen to how the other person responds. For some items, the person you address may not respond verbally.

7. You are about to end a phone call with Kimura-san from Aoi Shuppan. End the call appropriately.
8. You work for Ogaki Shokai. You have just taken a call from a representative of Aoi Shuppan, who has asked to speak to Kanda-san. After asking the person to wait, you were able to confirm that Kanda-san is available. You are just now returning to the phone. Thank Kimura-san for waiting and tell him that you'll get (literally, switch with) Kanda-san.
9. You are getting ready for a presentation. Explain to Yagi-bucho that the speakers (スピーカー) in room 405 are a little old and you can't hear them very well, and ask what should be done about it.

10. You are speaking to your *koohai*. Ask her to tell you when (a) she is finished; (b) the job is completed; (c) Kanda-san arrives; (d) she finds out the time of the meeting; (e) it gets difficult to use; (f) she starts (lit. becomes) feeling unwell.
11. Suggest to a close friend that he (a) try on a smaller one (shoes); (b) try on a larger one (jacket); (c) try on a more stylish one (glasses); (d) try on a more fashionable one (hat).
12. You are out shopping with a friend, looking at a certain item. Tell him that if it's expensive, you don't really want to buy it.
13. Tell a friend not to (a) eat too much; (b) think (about it) too much; (c) work too much; (d) drink too much; (e) use it too much; (f) buy too much.
14. Tell a *senpai* that you make it a habit to (a) study Japanese every day; (b) wake up at five a.m.; (c) go to Hokkaido every summer; (d) wear short sleeves in the fall.
15. Comment to a co-worker that (a) if you had known it was his birthday, you would have brought a present; (b) if you had consulted with the *bucho* this kind of thing wouldn't have happened; (c) if it hadn't been one person (doing it), it would have been completed by yesterday; (d) if we had looked at the schedule better, we wouldn't have gotten the time wrong; (e) if you had written a written a memo (for later) properly, you wouldn't have forgotten.
16. Ask a friend what kind of person Ikeda-kun's girlfriend is.

読んでみよう Contextualized reading

Consider the context provided and read the passage to answer the questions that follow.

(1) A work-related text message

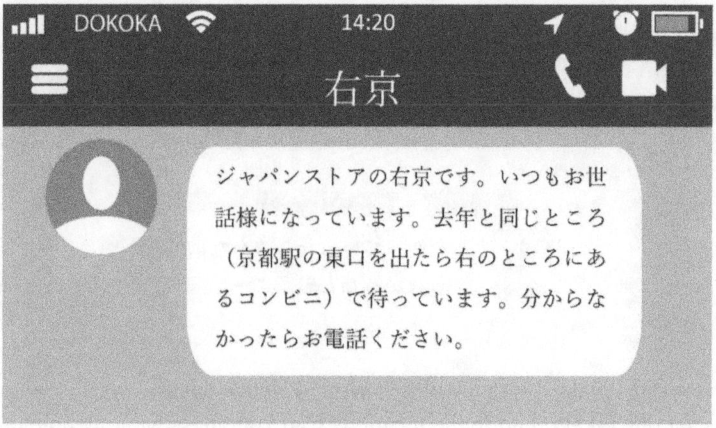
DOKOKA
14:20
右京
ジャパンストアの右京です。いつもお世話様になっています。去年と同じところ（京都駅の東口を出たら右のところにあるコンビニ）で待っています。分からなかったらお電話ください。

a. Who is the text message from?
b. Based on her greeting and speech style, what kind of relationship do you have with her?
c. Where is she waiting? Provide details.
d. What does she tell you to do? In what case?

(2) A hand-written memo attached to a container from your officemate Higashi-san.

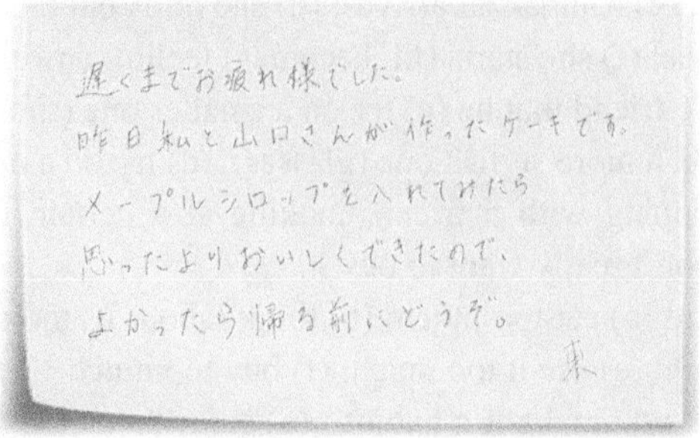

遅くまでお疲れ様でした。
昨日私と山口さんが作ったケーキです。
メープルシロップを入れてみたら
思ったよりおいしくできたので、
よかったら帰る前にどうぞ。
東

a. What assumption does she have about your work schedule?
b. What is in the container? Who made it? Why does she think it's tasty?
c. What does she urge you to do? When?

(3) A chat between Takako and Hiroshi:

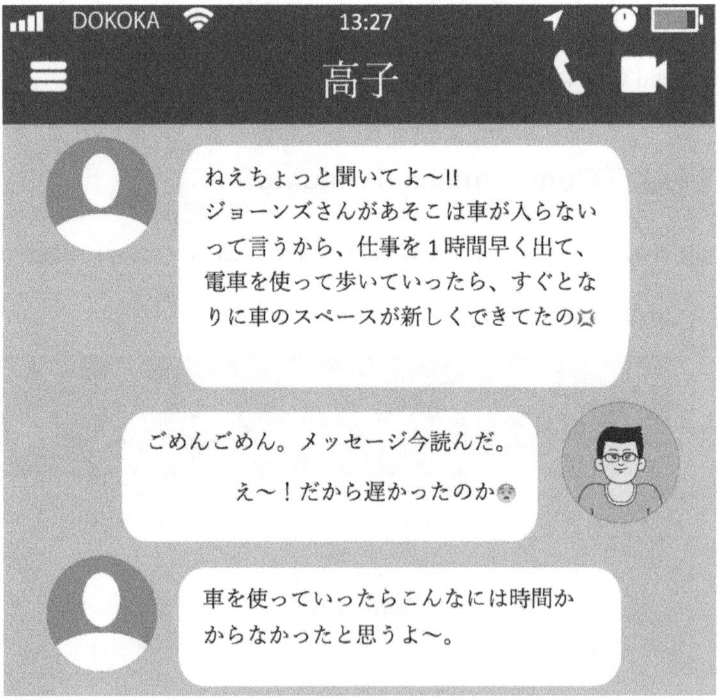

a. How did Takako get to the place? Why? Provide details.
b. What did Takako find in the location? Can you guess what feeling Takako wants to convey by using the 💢 emoji?
c. How does Hiroshi react to Takako? Why does he apologize first?
d. What would have saved Takako some time?

書き取り Dictation

Listen, imagine the context, repeat silently what you hear, then write it down.

1. ____。
2. ____。
3. ____。
4. ____。
5. ____。
6. ____。
7. ____。
8. ____。

書いてみよう Contextualized writing

Consider the context provided and compose the text according to the directions.

1. Write a short memo to thank your new officemate, Mr. Sakyo, for working late. Explain that the same work is entered (into the schedule) for tomorrow as well and tell him to call you in case there is something he's not sure about because you will leave (work) now (lit. from now).

2. Your client, Yamaguchi-san, will be visiting you in Kyoto. Write a short memo attached to a map of Kyoto, thanking him for being always kind to you. Tell him to use the map of Kyoto because you heard he was walking from the station.

3. Write a short memo attached to a book to your colleague, Ukyo-san. Tell her that it is the recipe book that Higashi-san tried cooking with and said was good. Invite her to try reading it on the train on the way back if she is not tired.

知ってる? What do you know?

Select the most appropriate option and write the letter on your answer sheet.

1. When Sentence ～たら is followed by a NON-PAST Sentence, the English equivalent of the ～たら form is ________. (BTS 1)

   a. 'no matter when'
   b. 'if' or 'when'
   c. 'if and only if'

2. When Sentence ～たら is followed by a PAST Sentence, the English equivalent of the ～たら form could be ________. (BTS 9, 12)

   a. 'if X had happened'
   b. 'when X happens'
   c. 'if and only if X happens'

3. When Sentence ～たら is followed by a PAST Sentence out of the speaker's control, the English equivalent of the ～たら form could be ________happened.' (BTS 9, 12)

   a. 'when X
   b. 'if X
   c. 'whenever X

4. You ask your coworker to tell you if there's something he doesn't understand.
   わからないことが_____________教えてください。(BTS 1)

   a. ですので
   b. あったの
   c. おありでしたら

5. When answering a business phone call, the first thing to do is ________. (BTS 2)

   a. ask who is calling
   b. acknowledge the relationship
   c. identify yourself

6. You ask if you should switch the call to the secretary.
   秘書______代わりましょうか。(BTS 3)

   a. に
   b. と
   c. へ

7. You offer to make the phone call instead of the division manager.
   部長____代わって、電話いたしましょうか。(BTS 3)

   a. に
   b. で
   c. が

8. You're wondering if you should wear your black slacks for the interview.
   黒いパンツ、__________行こうか。(BTS 4)

   a. 着て
   b. 履いて
   c. 重ねる

9. You're wondering how you should apologize to the section chief.
   __________でしょうか。(BTS 5)

   a. どう謝ったらいい
   b. 謝ったらいい
   c. 謝ったらどう

10. You suggest that your coworker wear something more formal to the wedding.
もっとフォーマルな服を ___________か。(BTS 5)
    a. 着ていったらいいです
    b. 着ていきましょう
    c. 着ていったらどうです

11. The verb 過ぎる attaches to _________. (BTS 6)
    a. *no* Nouns
    b. Adjective stems
    c. Verb roots

12. You're wondering what the TV commercial is for.
_______の薬じゃないでしょうか。(BTS 6)
    a. 飲みすぎ
    b. 飲みすぎる
    c. 飲みすぎた

13. You've been asked what you think of the results of the survey. You reply:
ちょっと________すぎると思う。(BTS 6)
    a. よ
    b. よい
    c. よく

14. You tell your friend that you decided to get a new cell phone.
新しい携帯を買う_________________。(BTS 7)
    a. ということにしました
    b. ことにしていました
    c. ことにしました

15. You tell your friend about your routine to wear casual clothes to work on Fridays.
毎週金曜日にカジュアルな服を着る_____________。(BTS 7)
    a. ということにします
    b. ことにしました
    c. ことにしています

16. Assuming that everyone will attend the reception, you suggest holding it at a certain hotel.
皆出る_____________あのホテルでしましょうか。(BTS 7)
    a. ことにして
    b. ということにして
    c. ことにしていて

17. You complain about having to wait at the restaurant for a table.

予約＿＿＿＿＿＿こんなに待つ必要はなかったけど……。(BTS 9)

a. したら
b. してたら
c. することにしたら

18. You comment on the perspective of the author of an article.

かなり＿＿＿＿＿＿考え方じゃないかと思う。(BTS 10)

a. 歴史的
b. 歴史的に
c. 歴史的な

19. You comment on an online course evaluation.

とっても＿＿＿＿＿＿書いてあるんじゃないですか。(BTS 10)

a. 積極的
b. 積極的に
c. 積極的な

20. You tell your friend that you have a dull stomachache.

お腹がちょっと＿＿＿＿してる。(BTS 14)

a. ズキズキ
b. ムカムカ
c. シクシク

21. When telling a story about a previous incident, you can use the non-past to _______. (BTS 15)

a. create a more vivid scenario
b. summarize the outcome
c. give background information

22. When listening to someone tell a story, you should use 相槌 to indicate that you ______. (BTS 15)

a. agree with the speaker
b. follow the story
c. wonder what will happen

23. Using the right language in business correspondence ______. (BTL 1)

a. puts people at ease
b. can make a difference in how readers view you as a representative of your company
c. both a and b

第 12 幕
Act 12

母(はは)が送(おく)ってくれたんだけど……。

My mom sent it to me . . .

◆ Scene 12-1 練習 Practice

理解練習 Comprehension practice

12-1-1C Who benefits? (BTS 1)

Indicate whether the information is being presented as benefitting the speaker (i.e., beneficial) or is not presented as benefitting the speaker (i.e., not beneficial).

Ex. 1.	☒ Beneficial	☐ Not beneficial
Ex. 2.	☐ Beneficial	☒ Not beneficial
3.	☐ Beneficial	☐ Not beneficial
4.	☐ Beneficial	☐ Not beneficial
5.	☐ Beneficial	☐ Not beneficial
6.	☐ Beneficial	☐ Not beneficial
7.	☐ Beneficial	☐ Not beneficial
8.	☐ Beneficial	☐ Not beneficial
9.	☐ Beneficial	☐ Not beneficial

実演練習 Performance practice

12-1-2P Thanking for the kind offer (BTS 1)

Whether you are talking to a client or a close friend, thank her for what she offers to do. Determine whether you are speaking to a client or a friend and adjust your language accordingly.

Ex. 1.

Client	この論文、よろしければお貸ししますよ。	I'll lend you this academic paper, if you'd like.
You	え?貸してくださるんですか。すみません。では遠慮なくお願いいたします。	What? You'll lend it to me? Thank you. Then I won't hold back; I'll take you up on it.

Ex. 2.

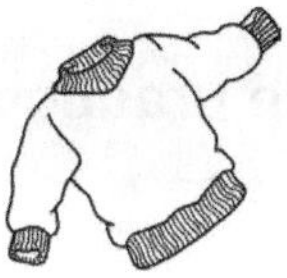

Friend	このセーター、よかったら貸すよ。	I'll lend you this sweater, if you'd like.
You	え、貸してくれるの?どうも。じゃ遠慮なく頼むよ。	What? You'll lend it to me? Thanks! Then I won't hold back; I'll take take you up on it.

3.	4.	5.	6.

7.	8.	9.	10.
	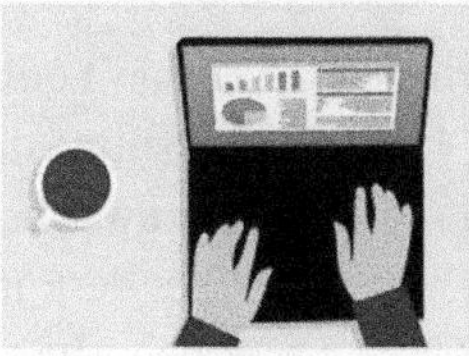		

12-1-3P Recognizing a kindness (BTS 1)

Your co-worker Suzuki-san is telling you about something that surprises you. If it's something that she did, assume that she did it for you and acknowledge the action as such in your response.

Ex. 1.

Suzuki-san	明日になりました。	It's going to be tomorrow.
You	え?明日になったんですか?	What? It's going to be tomorrow?

Ex. 2.

Suzuki-san	新しいのを買いました。	I bought a new one.
You	え?新しいのを買ってくれたんですか?	What? You bought a new one for me?

理解実演練習 Comprehension and performance practice

12-1-4CP Rephrasing (BTS 2)

You are listening to a friend, Nakajima-san, describe various people in her circle. After you listen to her speech, summarize the characterization or Nakajima-san's attitude about the person, using one of the expressions provided blow. Each expression is to be used only once.

Ex. 1.

Nakajima-san	課長が「やりたい人」って聞いたらね、インターンの青山くんっていう人がすぐ「やります！」って。いつもそう。誰よりも先に「やります！」って、すごく元気がいいの。	When the section chief asked "who wants to do it?" an intern called Aoyama-kun immediately said, "I'll do it!' He is always like that. Saying "I'll do it!" before anybody else, he is really full of energy.
You	へえ。積極的っていうこと？	Wow, you mean he is proactive?

Ex. 2.

Nakajima-san	どうも苦手だよね、うちの所長って。言っている事がよくわからないし、机の上が全然片付いてないし、あと、こっちの言うこと全然聞いてくれないの。	I can't quite handle her, our institute director. You never know what she is saying, and her desk is always messy. Oh, also, she never listens to what I'm saying.
You	へえ。嫌いっていうこと？	Wow, you mean you dislike her?

好き(す)き	嫌(きら)い	積極的(せっきょくてき)	消極的(しょうきょくてき)	
おしゃれ	優(やさ)しい	厳(きび)しい	怖(こわ)い	めんどくさい

12-1 腕試し Tryout

Tell a friend or acquaintance about a time that you needed help and someone did something for you.

◆ Scene 12-2 練習 Practice

理解練習 Comprehension practice

12-2-1C Whether or not… (BTS 4)

Match the number of the audio with the information that is unknown.

1.	Whether it is above or below average
2.	Whether it is necessary or not
3.	Whether he lives in Tokyo or not
4.	Whether it is his wife or not
5.	Whether it will be this month or not
6.	Whether she will come or not
7.	Whether it will be clean or not
8.	Whether it is tasty or not
9.	Whether it is in English or Japanese
10.	Whether it was sent yesterday or the day before

実演練習 Performance practice

12-2-2P Stating that they won't let you know (BTS 4)

Your supervisor tries to confirm Suzuki-san's plans. Tell her that Suzuki-san won't tell you.

Ex. 1.

Supervisor	鈴木さん、歯が痛いって言ってたね。よくなったかな?	Suzuki-san said her tooth hurt, didn't she. I wonder if it got better.
You	それがですね、よくなったかどうか、教えてくれないんです。	The thing is, she won't tell me if it got better or not.

Ex. 2.

Supervisor	鈴木さん、いとこが遊びに来ているって言ってたけど、まだいるのかな？	Suzuki-san said her cousin was visiting on vacation. I wonder if he's still here.
You	それがですね、まだいるかどうか、教えてくれないんです。	The thing is, she won't tell me if he's still here or not.

12-2-3P Suggesting you finish and be done with it (BTS 5)

When Sakai-san, a team member, suggests doing something, suggest doing it by the end of today and being done with it.

Ex. 1.

Sakai-san	棚の中の文房具、片付けましょうか。	Shall we tidy up the office supplies in the cabinet?
You	棚の中の文房具？そうですね。なるべく今日中に片付けちゃいましょう。	Office supplies in the cabinet? Yes. Let's try and finish tidying it up today.

Ex. 2.

Sakai-san	インターンの面接、しましょうか。	Shall we conduct the interviews for the interns?
You	インターンの面接？そうですね。なるべく今日中にしちゃいましょう。	Interviews for the interns? Yes, let's try and finish doing that today.

12-2 腕試し Tryout

Ask your Japanese friends/associates about Japanese food items that they are not sure if foreigners will like or not. Ask them to explain what they are.

◆ Scene 12-3 練習 Practice

理解練習 Comprehension practice

12-3-1C Whether or not… (BTS 6)

Match the number of the audio with the information that is unknown.

1.	What he said he's bad at
2.	How many people there are
3.	Which bookstore she bought it at
4.	What to do
5.	What the score was
6.	Who it is
7.	What his condition is
8.	When she's going to New York
9.	How long it will take
10.	What kind of Japanese food she likes
11.	How many minutes late it will be

実演練習 Performance practice

12-3-2P Saying you don't remember (BTS 6)

Your *senpai* asks you questions that you can't answer with any level of certainty. Tell him that you don't recall.

Ex. 1.

Senpai	開発部の人が受け取ったんですよね、この手紙。	Someone in the development division received it—this letter, right?
You	すみません。誰が受け取ったか、ちょっと覚えてないです。	Sorry. I don't recall exactly who received it.

Ex. 2.

Senpai	外国語いくつも知っているんでしょう?あのインターン。	She knows a number of foreign languages, right?—that intern.
You	すみません。いくつ知っているか、ちょっと覚えてないです。	Sorry. I don't recall exactly how many she knows.

12-3-3P Nudging for the conclusion (BTS 8)

Your friend Shota tends to stray from the topic. When he does, nudge him to get back to the topic by asking whether or not he acts on his initial comment.

Ex. 1.

Shota	犬をね、飼いたいかもしれない。やっぱり大きいのがいいな。あ、これ、シェパードか。頭良さそう。シェパードってね、子供にも優しいんだって。ほらあの、映画見た?シェパードがさ、子供の面倒見るの。	A dog—I might want to have a dog, you know. A big one will be good. Oh, this one. It's a shepherd, isn't it. Looks intelligent. You know, shepherds are gentle to children. Say, that movie, did you see it? The one where a shepherd dog looks after a child.
You	で、犬、飼うの?飼わないの?	So, are you going to get a dog or not?

Ex. 2.

Shota	彼女の好きなキャラのついた文房具をね、買ってあげたいかも。あ、これいいよね。あ、ペンじゃなくてシャーペンなんだ。それもいいかもしれないね。シャーペン、あると便利だよね、彼女さ、絵が上手だから。	Some stationery with a character my girlfriend likes—I might want to buy her some, you know. Look, this one is good, isn't it? Oh, it's not a pen, but it is a mechanical pencil. That might be good. Mechanical pencils come in handy, right? 'Cause she's, like, good at drawing.
You	で、文房具、買ってあげるの?あげないの?	So, are you going to buy some stationery for her or not?

12-3 腕試し Tryout

Ask your Japanese friends/associates to describe a person you have not met in terms of physical features. Then, try to identify the person in a group photograph.

◆ Scene 12-4 練習 Practice

理解練習 Comprehension practice

12-4-1C Who got it? (BTS 1, 9)

In each of the following, the speaker may be speaking of his/her own action, or of a third person's action to an in-group member. Listen and mark whether it was the speaker or the person mentioned by the speaker (an in-group member) that received the item.

Ex. 1. ☐ The speaker ☒ Suzuki-san
Ex. 2. ☒ The speaker ☐ Suzuki-san
3. ☐ The speaker ☐ Suzuki-san
4. ☐ The speaker ☐ Suzuki-san
5. ☐ The speaker ☐ Suzuki-san
6. ☐ The speaker ☐ Suzuki-san
7. ☐ The speaker ☐ Yagi-bucho
8. ☐ The speaker ☐ Yagi-bucho
9. ☐ The speaker ☐ Yagi-bucho
10. ☐ The speaker ☐ Yagi-bucho

12-4-2C Who did it? (BTS 1, 9)

In each of the following an action is mentioned. Some of these actions are followed by a giving verb (i.e., くれる or くださる) or a receiving verb (i.e., もらう or いただく). Listen and mark whether this main action is performed by the speaker or another person.

Ex. 1. ☐ The speaker ☒ Another person
Ex. 2. ☐ The speaker ☒ Another person
3. ☐ The speaker ☐ Another person
4. ☐ The speaker ☐ Another person
5. ☐ The speaker ☐ Another person
6. ☐ The speaker ☐ Another person
7. ☐ The speaker ☐ Another person
8. ☐ The speaker ☐ Another person
9. ☐ The speaker ☐ Another person

12-4-3C Isn't there a different reason? (BTS 11, 14)

Mark the option that accurately represents what the second speaker thinks.

Ex. 1.	☒ He is sick	☐ He isn't sick
Ex. 2.	☐ He has studied	☒ He hasn't studied
3.	☐ He ate too much	☐ He didn't eat too much
4.	☐ There's too much stuff	☐ There isn't too much stuff
5.	☐ He has too much to do	☐ He doesn't have too much to do
6.	☐ He has looked at the textbook	☐ He hasn't looked at the textbook
7.	☐ It's in his bag	☐ It's not in his bag

実演練習 Performance practice

12-4-4P Describing what happens when… (BTS 13)

Your supervisor, Maeda-san, mentions a situation. Confirm his thinking about what happens in that situation.

Ex. 1.

Maeda-san	もう1時過ぎましたけど、お腹空かない？	It's already after one. Aren't you getting hungry?
You	はい、1時を過ぎると確かにお腹が空きます。	Yes, once it's past one, I sure become hungry.

Ex. 2.

Maeda-san	腰が痛そうだけど、座って仕事するのはきついんじゃない？	It looks as if you have pain in the lower back. Isn't working sitting down hard?
You	はい、腰が痛いと確かに座って仕事するのはきついです。	Yes, once I have a lower backache, it's hard to work sitting down.

◆ Scene 12-5 練習 Practice

理解練習 Comprehension practice

12-5-1C She wants you to do it (BTS 17)

Mark whether the speaker is saying that Tanaka-san wants someone else to do it, or that someone wants Tanaka-san to do it.

Ex. 1.	☒ Tanaka-san wants someone to do it	☐ Someone wants Tanaka-san to do it
Ex. 2.	☐ Tanaka-san wants someone to do it	☒ Someone wants Tanaka-san to do it
3.	☐ Tanaka-san wants someone to do it	☐ Someone wants Tanaka-san to do it
4.	☐ Tanaka-san wants someone to do it	☐ Someone wants Tanaka-san to do it
5.	☐ Tanaka-san wants someone to do it	☐ Someone wants Tanaka-san to do it
6.	☐ Tanaka-san wants someone to do it	☐ Someone wants Tanaka-san to do it
7.	☐ Tanaka-san wants someone to do it	☐ Someone wants Tanaka-san to do it
8.	☐ Tanaka-san wants someone to do it	☐ Someone wants Tanaka-san to do it
9.	☐ Tanaka-san wants someone to do it	☐ Someone wants Tanaka-san to do it
10.	☐ Tanaka-san wants someone to do it	☐ Someone wants Tanaka-san to do it

実演練習 Performance practice

12-5-2P Stating a wish (BTS 9, 17)

You and your friend, Mei, have been talking about a common acquaintance, Yamada-san. At one point, Mei summarizes what you have been saying. Respond by stating it more explicitly as your wish.

Ex. 1.

Mei	ということは、山田さんにご家族に会ってもらいたいんだね?	So, that means you want Yamada-san to meet your family?
You	まあ、できたら家族に会って欲しいと思ってね。	Yeah, if possible, my wish is for Yamada-san to meet my family, you know.

Ex. 2.

Mei	ということは、山田さんにあちらに行ってもらいたくないんだね?	So, that means you don't want Yamada-san to go over there?
You	まあ、できたらあちらに行かないで欲しいと思ってね。	Yeah, if possible, my wish is for Yamada-san to not go over there, you know.

12-5-3P Criticizing the status quo (BTS 16)

When your associate, Okada-san, describes the current situation, express your objection.

Ex. 1.

Okada-san	今はまだちょっと練習不足かもしれません。	She still might not have practiced enough.
You	でも、練習不足のままだと、困りますよね。	But if she keeps not practicing enough it'll be a problem.

Ex. 2.

Okada-san	今はどっちかというとわかりにくいんじゃないでしょうか。	I wonder if it isn't hard to understand now.
You	でも、わかりにくいままだと、困りますよね。	But if it continues to be hard to understand, it'll be a problem.

12-5-4P Directing to stay as is (BTS 16)

You are leading an exercise class. When one of your students reports that they have done something, ask everybody to listen to you as/where they are.

Ex. 1.

Student	集まりました。	We've gathered.
You	はい、じゃあ、集まったままで、そのままでちょっと聞いてください。	Okay, then with everyone gathered, just as you are, please listen.

Ex. 2.

Student	右手を斜め前に出しました。	I put my right hand forward diagonally.
You	はい、じゃあ、右手を斜め前に出したままで、そのままでちょっと聞いてください。	Okay, then with your right hand put diagonally forward, just as you are, please listen.

12-5 腕試し Tryout

The next time a Japanese friend/associate complains about another person, restate what they are telling you in terms of what they want the person to do. For example, if someone complains that her son doesn't study, you might say もっと勉強(べんきょう)してほしいってことですか?

◆ Scene 12-6 練習 Practice

理解練習 Comprehension practice

12-6-1C What's going on? (BTS 18)

In the audio, you will hear three different utterances. Select the utterance that best matches the given context, all of which involve your friend, Yamada-san.

Ex. 1.	Yamada-san bought it for me.	☒ a	☐ b	☐ c
Ex. 2.	I had Yamada-san do it.	☐ a	☐ b	☒ c
3.	Yamada-san lent it to me.	☐ a	☐ b	☐ c
4.	I told Yamada-san.	☐ a	☐ b	☐ c
5.	I had Yamada-san send it.	☐ a	☐ b	☐ c
6.	I made it for Yamada-san.	☐ a	☐ b	☐ c
7.	I had Yamada-san begin.	☐ a	☐ b	☐ c
8.	Yamada-san looked it up for me.	☐ a	☐ b	☐ c
9.	I translated it for Yamada-san.	☐ a	☐ b	☐ c

実演練習 Performance practice

12-6-2P Volunteering and taking credit (BTS 18)

When Mizuta-san, a subordinate member of your group, mentions the issue that no one wants to do a certain task, agree to do it for the group as a favor.

Ex. 1.

Mizuta-san	だれも山田くんを迎えに行きたくないんですよ。	It's that no one wants to go pick up Yamada-kun.
You	しょうがないな。じゃあ、私が行ってあげる。	There is no other way, is there? Okay, I'll go for you all.

Ex. 2.

Mizuta-san	だれも大きなプレゼンをしたくないんですよ。	It's that no one wants to do the big presentation.
You	しょうがないな。じゃあ、私がしてあげる。	There is no other way, is there? Okay, I'll do it for you all.

12-6-3P Volunteering without overtly taking credit (BTS 1, 18)

Your supervisor, Kato-san, is concerned about a task not being done. Volunteer with confidence. Remember to use a humble form when the action engages someone higher up.

Ex. 1.

Kato-san	だれか家まで迎えに来てくれないかなあ。	I wonder if anyone would come pick me up at the house.
You	あ、私がお迎えに参ります。お任せください。	Oh, I'll come pick you up. Please leave it to me.

Ex. 2.

Kato-san	だれかここ片付けてくれないかなあ。	I wonder if anyone would tidy it up here.
You	あ、私が片付けます。お任せください。	Oh, I'll tidy it up. Please leave it to me.

12-6-4P Wanting to help (BTS 18)

Taguchi-san, your project team leader, is not around, and you are talking to Mizuta-san, a team member that you are close to. When Mizuta-san admires what he thinks Taguchi-san has done, gently mention how you wish you could help.

Ex. 1.

Mizuta-san	さすが田口さん。面倒なお客様にも丁寧に説明したんだってね。	True to his reputation, Taguchi-san explained carefully even to the bothersome customer, I hear!
You	そうなんです。私が代わってして差し上げたいけどそれもちょっとね。	Yeah. I want to help and do it in his place, but that won't work either, you know.

Ex. 2.

Mizuta-san	さすが田口さん。かなりのレポートを１日で書いたんだってね。	True to his reputation, Taguchi-san wrote a substantial report in one day, I hear!
You	そうなんです。私が代わって書いて差し上げたいけど、それもちょっとね。	Yeah. I want to help and write it in his place, but that won't work either, you know.

◆ Scene 12-7 練習 Practice

読み練習 Reading practice

12-7-1R Someone does you a favor

Complete the following sentences with appropriate verbs of giving from the selection.

a. 教えてくださいました。	d. 来てくれました
b. 教えてくれました	e. 見てくださいました
c. 見に来てくれました	f. 書いてくれました

Ex. 1. 先生が新しい漢字を＿＿a＿＿。

Ex. 2. 男の子が教室まで＿＿d＿＿。

3. 小さな女の子がゲームのモンスターの強さと弱さについて＿＿＿＿＿＿。
4. ジョーンズ先生が英語の勉強を＿＿＿＿＿＿。
5. たくさんの知らない人が私のパフォーマンスを＿＿＿＿＿＿。
6. 小さな男の子がメールを＿＿＿＿＿＿。

12-7-2R Making logical assumptions

Select the most logical assumption for each of the statements below.

a. 英語も分からない	e. まだ学校にも来ていない
b.「あれ」を見てしまった	f. まだ行ったことがない
c. あの漢字も知らない	g. まだ会ったことがない
d. 人前で話すのも好きじゃない	

Ex. 1. 教室に来てないということは＿＿e＿＿ということですね。

Ex. 2. プレッシャーに弱いということは、＿＿d＿＿ということですね。

3. 勉強ができないということは、＿＿＿＿＿＿ということですね。
4. この漢字が分からないということは、＿＿＿＿＿＿ということですね。
5. あのキャラクターが大きいか小さいか知らないということは、＿＿＿＿＿＿ということですね。
6. 教会についてあまり知らないということは、＿＿＿＿＿＿ということですね。
7. あの教室に入ってしまったということは、＿＿＿＿＿＿ということですね。

12-7 書き練習 Writing practice

文字練習 Symbol practice

Use the Symbol Practice sheets in Appendix A to practice kanji characters #109-117 for Scene 12-7.

12-7-3W Making a request with an embedded yes/no question

Complete the following requests using embedded yes/no questions.

Ex. 1.	＿＿大きい＿＿ か ＿どう(小さい)＿ か分からない。	big or small
Ex. 2.	イスラム教について ＿＿知ってる＿＿ か ＿どう(知らない)＿ か聞いてください。	knows or not
3.	これが＿＿＿＿＿＿か＿＿＿＿＿＿か聞いてみてくれる?	kanji or not
4.	ここが＿＿＿＿＿＿か＿＿＿＿＿＿か聞いてくださいませんか?	classroom or not
5.	このキャラクターが＿＿＿＿＿＿か＿＿＿＿＿＿か教えてくれない?	strong or weak
6.	ここで＿＿＿＿＿＿か＿＿＿＿＿＿か聞いて来ようよ。	okay to study or not

◆ Scene 12-8 練習 Practice

読み練習 Reading practice

12-8-1R Verbs of giving and receiving

Match each phrase on the left with a sentence on the right that completes it.

Ex. 1.	部長に来週のミーティングのアジェンダについて	___e___	a. 教えていただきました。
Ex. 2.	社長が長い間会社で	___d___	b. チェックしてくれました。
3.	会社の部下が明日は雪なのかどうか	______	c. 見てもらいました。
4.	同じビルにいた男の子に今雨なのかどうか外を	______	d. 待っていてくださいました。
5.	外国語の先生に留学プログラムについて	______	e. 短く話していただきました。
6.	クラスメートが昨日の英語のアサイメントのことを	______	f. 教えてくれました。

12-8-2R Questions with embedded information

Select the appropriate question word to complete each of the statements.

a. だれ	e. どこ
b. 何分ぐらい	f. 何時
c. 何だった	g. 何か月
d. どれぐらい	h. どうして

Ex. 1. テーブルの長さが___d___か分かりますか？

Ex. 2. 社長が帰って来ないのが___h___かメールには書いてありますか？

3. 語学に強い大学が______か知っていますか？

4. 女の人に弱いマンガのキャラクターって______か知ってる？

5. 明日の雨が雪になるのは______かチェックしてもらいたいんですけど……。

6. 留学のプログラムが______か教えてくれますか？

7. 会社まで歩いて行ったら______かだれか知らない？

8. もっと早くに知っておきたかったことって______か教えてもらいたいんですけど……。

12-8 書き練習 Writing practice

文字練習 Symbol practice

Use the Symbol Practice sheets in Appendix A to practice kanji characters #118-126 for Scene 12-8.

12-8-3W Greetings

Listen to each greeting and fill in the missing information in the appropriate cell.

Ex. 1. 中村社長 ___長い間___ありがとうございました。	4. ____________ ____________でしたけど__________ なりました。
Ex. 2. 山田部長 ___お元気___でいらっしゃいますか？	5. ____________ いつも ______________________ ありがとうございます。
3. ____________ この間は______________________ ありがとうございました。	6. ____________ 先日はあいにく ______________________ね。

◆ Scene 12-9 練習 Practice

読み練習 Reading practice

12-9-1R Things I would like you to do…

Choose the appropriate expression for each of the following requests.

Ex. 1.	学校のアサイメントで___g___本があるんだけど……。	a. やってほしい
Ex. 2.	朝に___a___仕事があるんだけど……。	b. 世話してほしい
3.	お昼休みに______人がいるんだけど……。	c. 出てほしい
4.	今晩______デザートがあるんだけど……。	d. 入ってほしい
5.	来週______部会があるんだけど……。	e. 休んでほしい
6.	安田さんに______インターンがいるんだけど……。	f. 聞いてほしい
7.	名前を______人がいるんだけど……。	g. 読んでほしい
8.	ブライアンに______サークルがあるんだけど……。	h. 会ってほしい
9.	今週ちょっと______日があるんだけど……。	i. 作ってほしい

12-9-2R Shall I volunteer?

For each of the situations below, choose the appropriate service that you are going to provide from the selection below.

a. 私がみんなに時間のこと教えてあげようか?	e. 私が何か作って来てあげようか?
b. 私がレポート書いてあげようか?	f. 私が車出してあげようか?
c. 私が英語の部分を読んでさしあげようか?	g. 私が何か買って来てさしあげようか?
d. 私が電話かけてあげようか?	

Ex. 1.	部長ってもしかしたら朝ご飯食べてないんじゃないの?	g
Ex. 2.	モリスさん、もしかすると土日も休みがないんじゃないの?	b
3.	ブライアン、もしかすると毎日歩いて来てるんじゃないの?	___
4.	今晩のホームパーティーってもしかしたら晩ご飯出ないんじゃないの?	___

5. 社長ってもしかしたら英語が分からないんじゃないの？ ______
6. 安田さんってもしかしたら朝に弱いからまだ来てないんじゃないの？ ______
7. 昼休みってもしかしたら1時までなんじゃないの？ ______

12-9-3R Warning with consequences

Select the likely consequence for each of the conditions below. You may use each option only once.

a. 土日もやることになっちゃうよ。	e. 帰るのが遅くなっちゃうよ。
b. すぐに疲れちゃうよ。	f. 外食することになってしますよ。
c. すぐにだめになってしまいますよ。	g. だれも買ってくれなくなってしまいますよ。
d. みんな食べに行ってしまいますよ。	

Ex. 1. 朝からしないと______e______
Ex. 2. 買ってもいいけど、ただ安いのだと______c______
3. 少し休まないと__________________
4. 昼休み前に言っておかないと__________________
5. 晩ご飯作っておかないと__________________
6. 毎日やらないと__________________
7. 安くないと__________________

書き練習 Writing practice

文字練習 Symbol practice

Use the Symbol Practice sheets in Appendix A to practice kanji characters #127-133 for Scene 12-9.

12-9-4W Rephrasing statements

Rephrase each of the statements on the left using a *kanji* that has the opposite meaning.

Ex. 1.	大きくなくて作りやすいですね。	小さくて 作りやすいですね。
Ex. 2.	右じゃないといいですね。	左だと いいですね。
Ex. 3.	遅かったらだめですね。	早くなかったら だめですね。
4.	長くないとだめですね。	________だめですね。
5.	午前中からじゃなかったらいいですね。	________いいですね。
6.	多くなかったらだめですね。	________だめですね。
7.	高くなくていいですね。	________いいですね。
8.	上手だといいですね。	________いいですね。
9.	子どもじゃなくてよかったですね。	________よかったですね。
10.	男の人だったらだめですね。	________だめですね。
11.	仕事に行かなくてよかったですね。	仕事を________よかったですね。
12.	昼休みの後じゃないといいですね。	________いいですね。

◆ 評価 Assessment

Answer sheet templates are provided in Appendix B for the Assessment sections.

聞いてみよう Listening comprehension

Read the context, listen to the audio, and then answer the questions based on what you hear. If you hear something unfamiliar, rely on what you know to answer the question.

1. Ichiro is talking to his cousin, who is visiting with him.

    a. What does Ichiro offer to do?
    b. What does Ichiro say he won't do?
    c. What does Ichiro's cousin say she will do?

2. Suzuki-sensei came to help her fellow teacher, Kitagawa-sensei. He is moving into a new apartment not too far from her house.

    a. What does Suzuki-sensei ask?
    b. What does Kitagawa-sensei ask Suzuki-sensei to do?

3. Kitagawa-sensei's new apartment is looking better. Suzuki-sensei is getting ready to go.

    a. What reason does Suzuki-sensei give for coming over?
    b. What does Kitagawa-sensei say was a help?
    c. What does Kitagawa-sensei offer to do for Suzuki-sensei?
    d. What reasons does Suzuki-sensei give for refusing?
    e. What does Suzuki-sensei tell Kitagawa-sensei to do?

4. A visiting professor from Japan is talking to Takashi about a mascot character after seeing it on Brian's cell phone strap.

    a. What is the professor checking on?
    b. What does Takashi ask the professor?
    c. How does the professor respond?
    d. Why does Takashi think Kumamoto is a nice place?

5. Sakamoto-sensei heard that Professor Smith, a visiting scholar from the US, likes Japanese cartoons.

    a. What did Professor Smith do when he was a child?
    b. What two things happened as a result of this?
    c. How old was Professor Smith when this happened? What grade was he in?

6. Eri and her *senpai* at school, Ōmori-san, are at a pet shop on the way back from doing some errands for their professor.

   a. How does Eri describe the dog's physical appearance?
   b. In addition to it being cute, what else does Eri think about this dog?
   c. What does Ōmori-san think about the dog?
   d. What does Eri ask Ōmori-san?
   e. How does Ōmori-san respond? What reason does Ōmori-san give for his answer?
   f. What reason does Eri give for not keeping a dog?

7. Eri and her *senpai*, Ōmori-san, are talking as they walk back to the university after their errands.

   a. What specifically does Eri not like?
   b. According to Eri, what is the effect of this way of speaking on men? Older women? Younger women?

8. Ichiro is talking to Ōtomo-san, a fellow aikidoist, about her family.

   a. Describe Ōtomo-san's siblings.
   b. What did Ōtomo-san's parents say as a joke?

9. Sasha and Kanda-san are at a lobby of a hotel, waiting for their appointment.

   a. What is Sasha impressed by?
   b. What comment does Kanda-san make about the hotel?
   c. What guess does Kanda-san make about this hotel?
   d. What did Sasha hear?

10. Yabunaka-san is a salesperson at an electronic store. His supervisor, who has been talking to a customer, summons him toward them.

    a. What does Yabunaka-san's supervisor ask him to do? Who will he do this for?
    b. Why does Yabunaka-san tell the customers to wait?
    c. What does Yabunaka-san say he will do when he comes back?

11. Yamamoto-san from Aoi Publishing asks Sasha about Kanda-san at a reception.

    a. What does Yamamoto-san ask about Kanda-san?
    b. What does Yamamoto-san ask about Kanda-san's wife?
    c. What information does Sasha provide about Kanda-san's wife? What information is she unable to provide?
    d. According to Sasha, what did Kanda-san say? What is the reason for this situation?

12. At the end of a long workshop, the workshop leader says he wants to conclude the workshop with some relaxation exercises.

    a. Before the relaxation exercises begin, what does the workshop leader tell everyone?
    b. What does the leader tell everyone to do to start the relaxation exercises?

使ってみよう Dry run

For each of the following, listen to the audio and respond to what was said based on the context.

1. Tell a co-worker (a) you had Tomoda-san (the intern) go to the train station to meet her; (b) Mizuno-sensei, from Tokyo University, lent it to you; (c) Tomoda-san cleaned up; (d) Mizuno-sensei brought them.
2. You are speaking to a *senpai* at work. There is a convenience store located nearby.
3. You are speaking to a *koohai* at work. The location he is asking about is not far. You think it's about five minutes away by car.
4. When a friend suggests 5 p.m. as a possibility, reply that it's fine, it's just that when it gets to be around 5 p.m. there are a lot of people.
5. You just received a phone call. When your *senpai* asks what is going on, summarize the content of the phone call as follows: (a) Yamada-san will not be coming; (b) next week is not possible; (c) it has been decided that he will take one day off; (d) it has been decided that he will go to Hokkaido for about three days on business; (e) she wants you to talk to the division chief; (f) he wants you to change places with Suzuki-san.
6. Suggest to a friend—requesting confirmation—that the reason for his difficulties is that he didn't practice enough.
7. A friend has reminded you of something that you had forgotten, but still might be able to do something about. Tell him that you forgot.
8. A friend has reminded you of something that you had forgotten, and it's now too late to do anything about. Tell her that you forgot.
9. When a friend asks what's going on, explain that you kind of ended up (a) eating too much; (b) getting stiff shoulders; (c) oversleeping; (d) switching with Ishikawa-kun.
10. You are speaking to a *koohai*. You would like the room kept as it is.
11. When a friend of yours asks about an item, tell him that (a) you gave it to Tanaka-san; (b) Tanaka-san gave it to you.

For each of the following, say something that would be appropriate in the given context. Then compare what you said to the sample, and listen to how the other person responds.

12. Ask a friend if he knows (a) if it will be two o'clock or three o'clock; (b) if Tanaka-san will come (for our benefit) or not; (c) if Suzuki-san is good at math; (d) whether or not it ended up (lit. became) that Ikeda-kun will study abroad in the US.
13. Ask a co-worker if she knows (a) who will come (for our benefit); (b) how many copies Ikebe-san made for us; (c) what the name of Division Chief Yagi's oldest child was; (d) which room the eleven o'clock meeting is in.
14. Apologize to Mizuno-sensei for having her come so far.
15. When Murata-san mentions how he's having trouble getting ahold of Nakatani-san, suggest the possibility that Nakatani-san might be on a business trip.
16. Express to a work *senpai* your hope that (a) the weather clears up; (b) she (the intern) comes quickly (for our benefit); (c) it doesn't rain; (d) it's not tomorrow.
17. Tell the intern to please do this after he's finished all of that.

読んでみよう Contextualized reading

Read the following texts and answer the questions that follow.

(1) Sasha updated her status on social media.

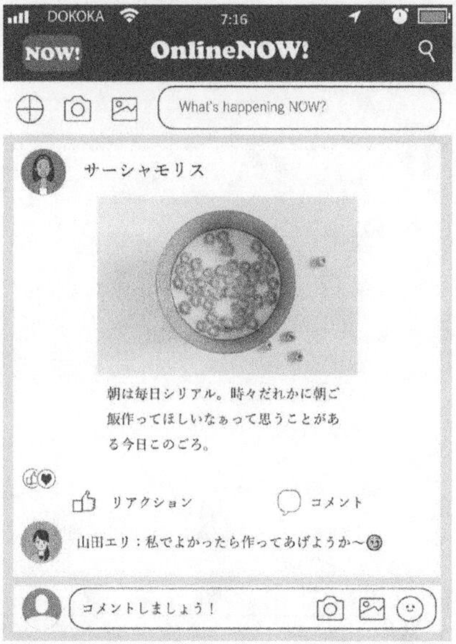

a. How often does she eat cereal? When?
b. What wish does she have?
c. How does her friend Eri react to the post?

(2) Sasha updated her status on social media again.

DOKOKA
18:23
NOW!
OnlineNOW!
What's happening NOW?
サーシャモリス
会社の人に昼ご飯作ってあげたら、おいしいって言ってくれた 明日も作ってあげようかな。また食べてくれるといいなぁ。
リアクション
コメント
山田エリ：だれに作ってあげたの～？もしかしていい人❤？？
コメントしましょう！

a. What did she make? For whom? What reaction did she get?
b. What is she going to do tomorrow? What wish does she have?
c. What questions does her friend Eri have?

(3) Sasha updated her status on social media for the third time on the same day.

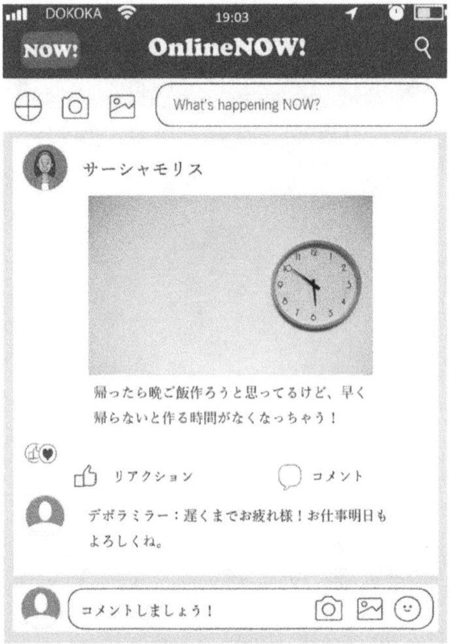

a. What is she planning to do when she finishes her work?
b. Why is she in a hurry?
c. Who is Debra Miller? How do you know?

書き取り Dictation

Listen, imagine the context, repeat silently what you hear, then write it down.

1. ____。
2. ____。
3. ____。
4. ____。
5. ____。
6. ____。
7. ____。
8. ____。

書いてみよう Contextualized writing

1. (Typing) Write a blog about today's weather (pictured below). Describe this morning's weather. Add that your (describe yourself as not a morning person) class starts in the afternoon (lit. from lunch time) and make a wishful comment that it doesn't turn into snow…

2. (Typing) Write a short blog about the dinner you made. Report that today is your day off and you tried making ramen for dinner with everyone in the soccer club. Add that it is especially tasty when you add an egg.

3. You are in Kyoto on a study abroad program. Write a postcard to your former teacher, Yasuda-sensei. Ask her politely how she is doing. Tell her that you are in Kyoto now on study abroad and are studying hard every day. Tell her that there are many things such as *kanji* you still don't know, but you love Japan. Thank her for teaching you Japanese. Invite her to use the postcard in the classroom.

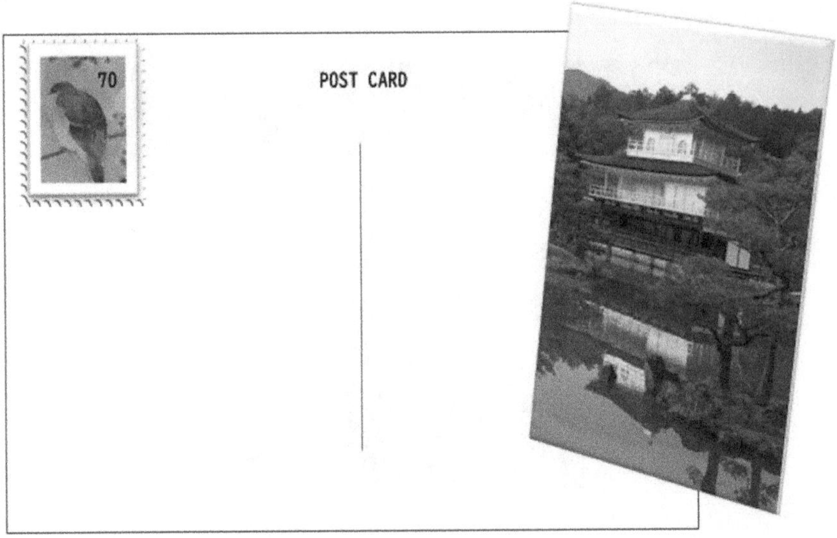

知ってる? What do you know?

Select the most appropriate option and write the letter on your answer sheet.

1. You've been asked who gave you the new alarm clock. You reply:
   姉(あね)が__________。(BTS 1)

   a. くれました
   b. くださいました

2. You've been asked who gave you the new textbook. You reply:
   先生(せんせい)が__________。(BTS 1)

   a. くれました
   b. くださいました

3. You've been asked who made the cake for your classmates. You reply:
   先生(せんせい)の奥(おく)さんが作(つく)って__________。(BTS 1)

   a. くれた
   b. くださった

4. You've been asked who checked your Japanese. You reply:
谷先生(たにせんせい)にチェックして＿＿＿＿＿＿。(BTS 1, 9, 18)

a. くださった
b. いただいた
c. あげた

5. You're wondering whom to ask to help out.
誰(だれ)に手伝(てつだ)って＿＿＿＿＿＿＿＿か。(BTS 9, 17, 18)

a. さしあげましょう
b. ほしいでしょう
c. もらいましょう

6. You offer to lend your textbook to your friend.
私(わたし)の教科書(きょうかしょ)、貸(か)して＿＿＿＿＿。(BTS 9, 18)

a. さしあげよう
b. もらおう
c. あげよう

7. You'd like to have someone take a look at a draft copy for errors, but you're not sure who to ask.
これ、ちょっと＿＿＿＿＿＿＿んだけど……。(BTS 9, 17)

a. 見(み)てほしい
b. 見(み)たい
c. 見(み)せてもらいたい

8. You ask about what you have concluded based on what you just heard.
一(ひと)つもない＿＿＿＿＿＿＿＿？(BTS 2)

a. というもの
b. ことなの
c. っていうこと

9. You haven't yet decided whether you'll rent a car or not.
レンタカー＿＿＿＿＿＿＿かまだ決(き)めてない。(BTS 4)

a. 借(か)りることにする
b. 借(か)りるかどう
c. 借(か)りますか借(か)りません

10. You lament the fact that you ended up eating the whole pint of ice cream.
全部食べて____________________。(BTS 5)

a. すぎました
b. しまいました
c. おきました

11. You've been asked if you know who will be coming to the meeting. You reply:
誰が________わかりませんねえ。(BTS 4, 6)

a. 来るか
b. 来るかどうか
c. 来るか来ないか

12. Particle さ at the end of a Sentence is similar to Particle ______. (BTS 7)

a. か
b. よ
c. ね

13. Particle さ at the end of a phrase is similar to Particle ______. (BTS 7)

a. か
b. よ
c. ね

14. When you use で as a question at the beginning of a Sentence, you're asking _____. (BTS 8)

a. 'and so then?'
b. 'how about that?'
c. 'why is that?'

15. You suggest going to a cafe near the train station.
駅の________カフェへ行こう。(BTS 10)

a. 近いの
b. 近くの
c. い

16. You tell your roommate not to worry, that it's not the food. It's that you just don't feel like eating.
______食べたくないんです。(BTS 11)

a. だって
b. それで
c. ただ

17. You've been asked why you don't want to take a history course. You reply:

歴史______弱いから。(BTS 12)

a. が
b. に
c. は

18. You tell your friend that when you drink coffee you get a queasy stomach.

コーヒーを___________とお腹が ムカムカする。(BTS 13)

a. 飲む
b. 飲んだ
c. 飲もう

19. You tell your homestay brother that when you went to the library, all the new students had gathered there.

図書館に_____________、新しい学生が皆集まってた。(BTS 13)

a. 行くと
b. 行ったから
c. 行ったら

20. The「んじゃない」in ちょっと失礼なんじゃないの？ is used to _________. (BTS 14)

a. seek confirmation
b. offer a reason
c. express disagreement

21. You are the youngest of three children. How would you describe your second-born older sister to your colleague? (BTS 15)

a. 下のお姉さん
b. 二番目の姉
c. 下の姉

22. You tell your roommate that it's okay for her to stay dressed casually.

カジュアル________ままでいいよ。(BTS 16)

a. な
b. の
c. に

23. You find out that it's been decided that you'll return to China after graduation.

中国に帰る______________________________。(BTS 19)

a. ことになっている

b. ということです

c. ことにしました

24. You're wondering if a possible reason your friend is late might be that the flight was delayed.

__________フライトは遅れたのかもしれない。(BTS 20)

a. きっと

b. もしかしたら

c. たしかに

25. Which of the following is <u>not</u> used to connect two Sentences in written style? (BTL 1)

a. ～く form

b. ～て form

c. ～ます form

Appendix A: 文字練習 (もじれんしゅう) Symbol practice

漢字 (かんじ)

Instruction

For each symbol, study the overall shape (top left) and stroke order, then complete every box to the right of it.

Act 7

#1

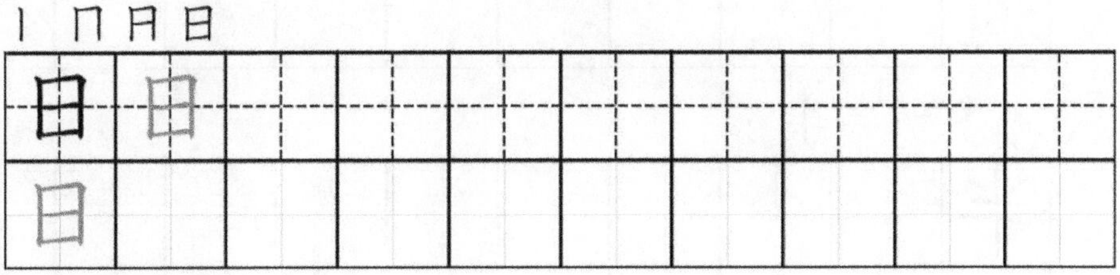

#2

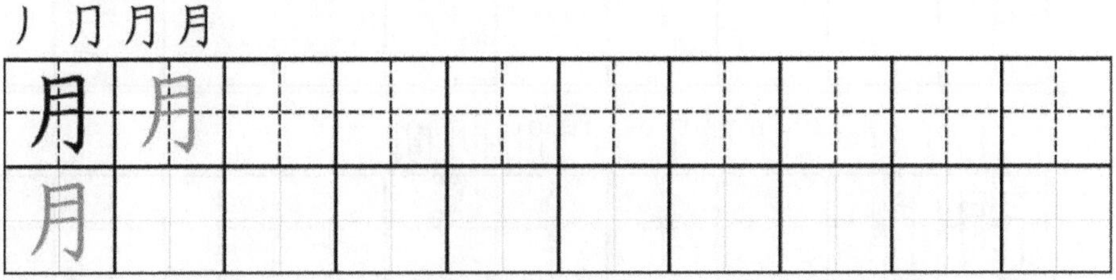

#3

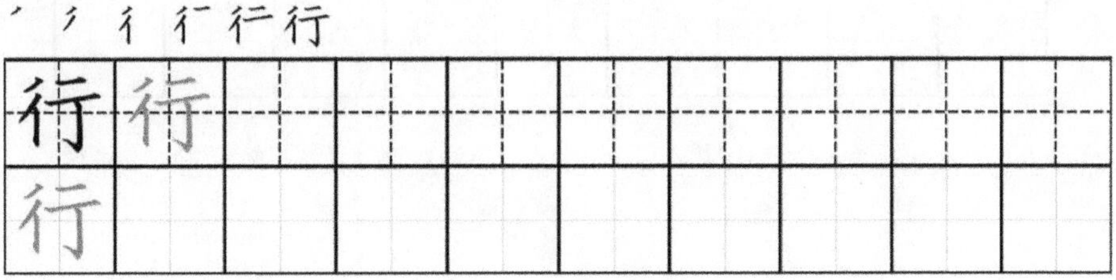

#4 一 丆 冖 亚 平 来 来

来 来 来

#5 丨 冂 月 日 日一 日十 日土 日圭 時 時

時 時 時

#6 丿 亻 亻一 亻丆 伂 佝 何

何 何 何

#7 丶 丷 䒑 兰 半

半 半 半

#8 丨 𠃍 户 户 户 門 門 門 閂 間 間 間

間 間 間

Act 8

#9 一 十 才 木 本

本 本

本

#10 ノ 人

人 人

人

#11 一

一 一

一

#12 丨 冂 冂 円

円 円

円

#13 ノ 𠂉 𠂉 𠂉 𠂉 年

年 年

年

#14 一 二

二 二

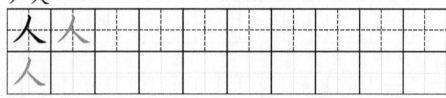

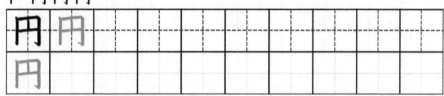

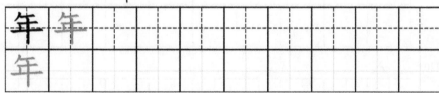

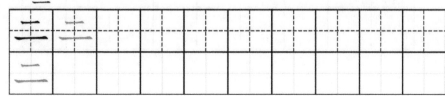

二

#15 一 二 三

三 三 三

#16 丨 冂 冂 冋 四

四 四 四

#17 一 丆 万 五

五 五 五

#18 丶 亠 六 六

六 六 六

#19 一 七

七 七 七

#20 丿 八

八 八 八

Appendix A

#21 丿 九

九 九
九

#22 一 十

十 十
十

#23 一 丆 丆 丙 百 百

百 百
百

#24 丿 二 千

千 千
千

#25 一 丆 万

万 万
万

#26 丨 冂 月 月 目

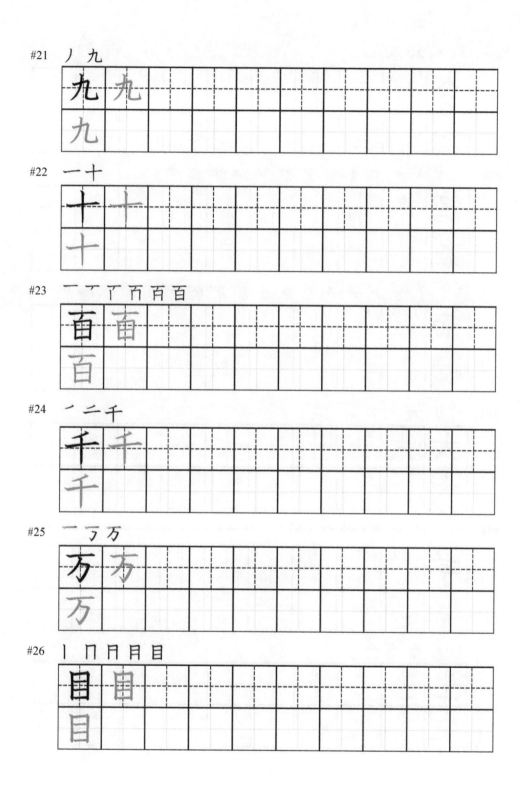

目 目
目

#27 ノ 人 𠆢 今

今 今
今

#28 丶 亠 亠 亖 亖 言 言 訁 訂 訂 訂 語 語 語

語 語
語

#29 一 厂 厂 厂 历 盾 盾 厚 原 原 原 原 原 原 原 願 願 願 願

願 願
願

#30 一 ナ 大

大 大
大

#31 丶 丷 ⺍ ⺍ 𭕄 学 学 学

学 学
学

#32 ノ 𠂉 牛 牛 生

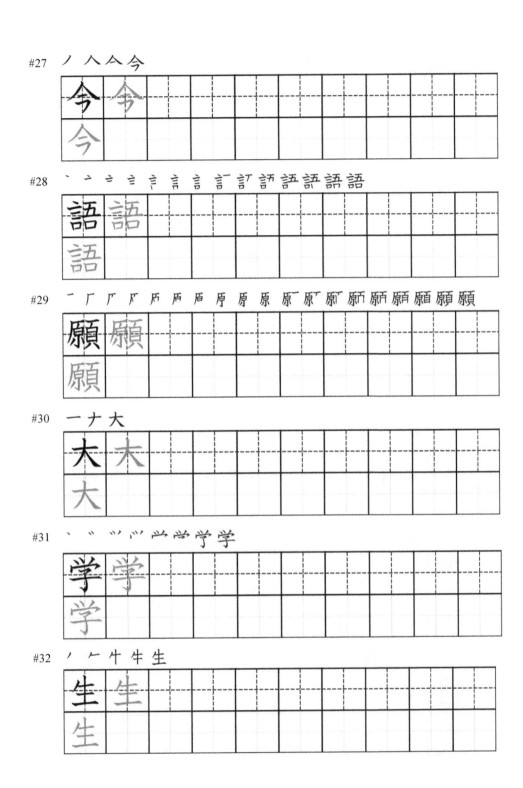

生 生
生

#33 先

先 先

先

Act 9

#34 週

週 週

週

#35 火

火 火

火

#36 曜

曜 曜

曜

#37 男

男 男

男

#38 水

水 水

水

#39 一 十 才 木

木 木
木

#40 ノ 𠆢 亼 今 仒 全 余 金

金 金
金

#41 一 十 土

土 土
土

#42 く 女 女

女 女
女

#43 乛 了 子

子 子
子

#44 一 十 才 木 木' 杧 杧 校 校 校

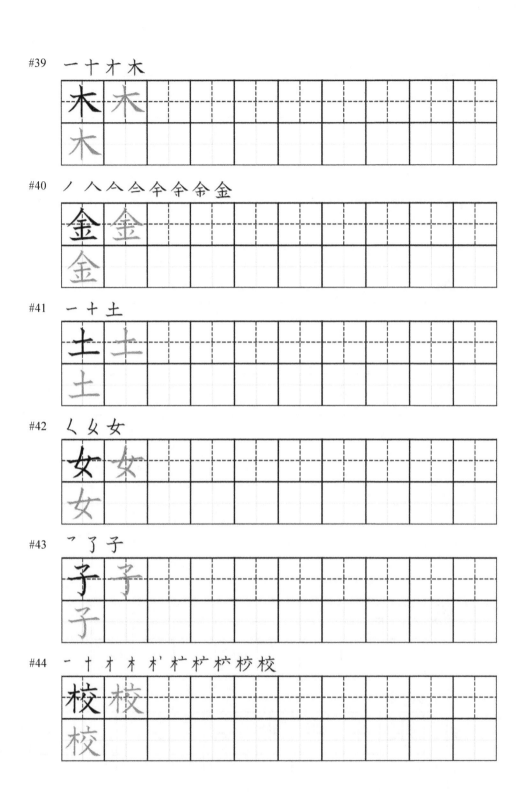

校 校
校

#45 丶 亠 亠 亡 亩 亩 亭 高 高 高 高

高 高
高

#46 丿 川 川

川 川
川

#47 丨 卜 上

上 上
上

#48 ノ ク タ タ 名 名

名 名
名

#49 丶 丷 䒑 䒑 前 前 前 前 前

前 前
前

#50 ノ 八 分 分

分 分
分

#51 一 丅 下

下 下 下

#52 丨 𠃊 戶 戶 門 門 門 門 閂 閅 閈 閌 聞 聞

聞 聞 聞

#53 一 十 才 木 村 村 村

村 村 村

#54 丶 丿 𡿨 州 州 州

州 州 州

#55 丶 亠 亣 立 立

立 立 立

#56 丨 山 山

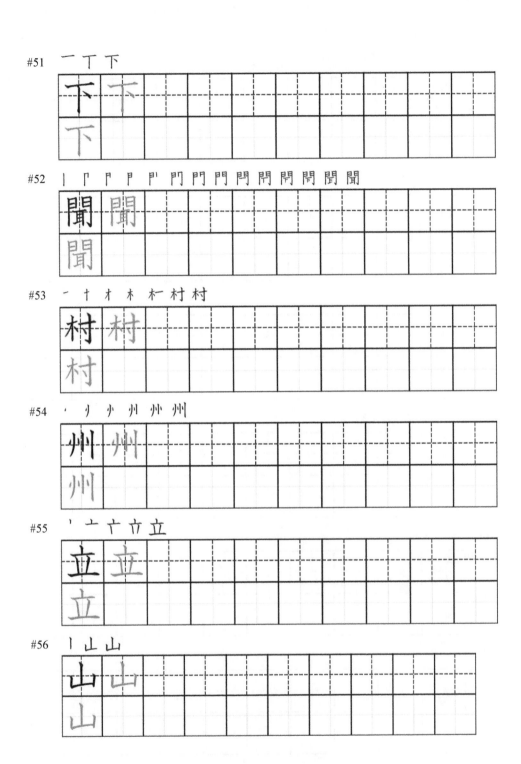

山 山 山

#57

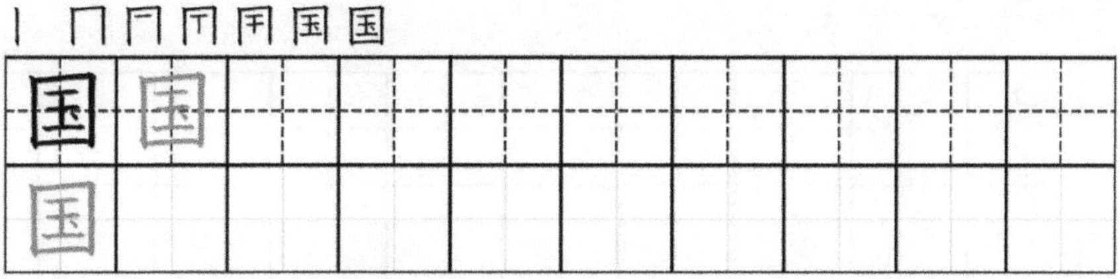

#58

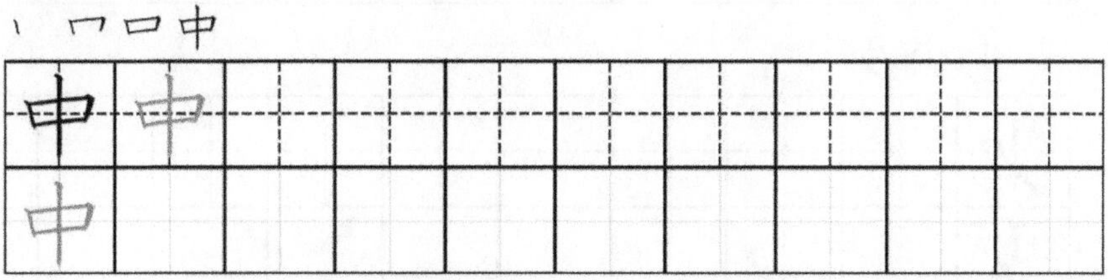

Act 10

#59

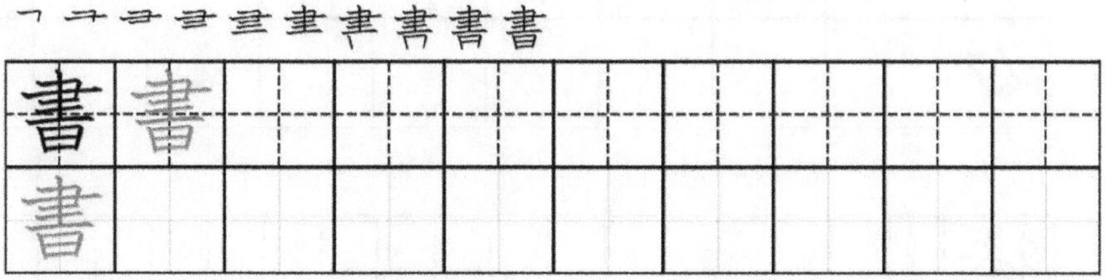

#60

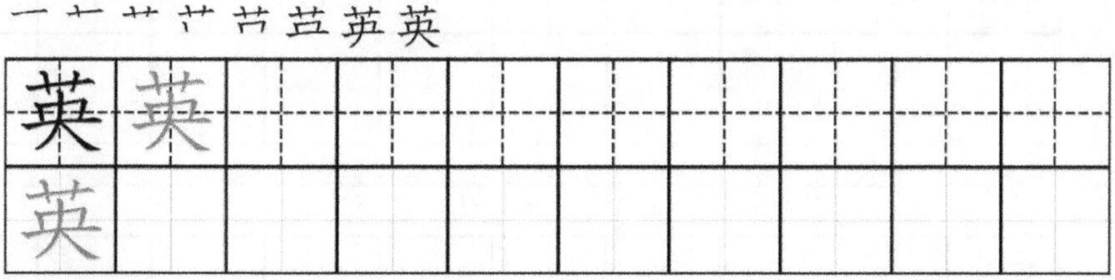

#61

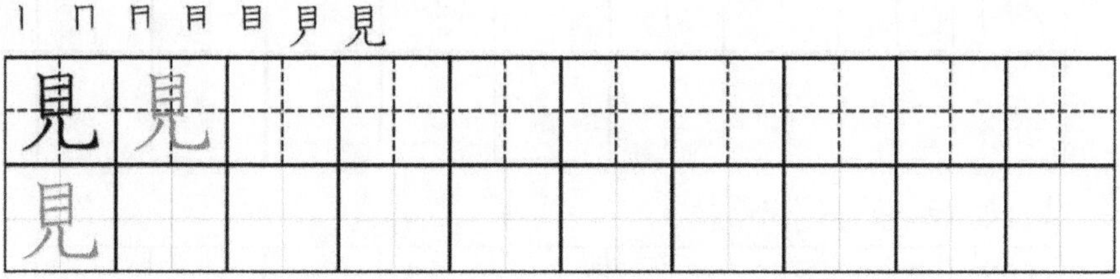

#62

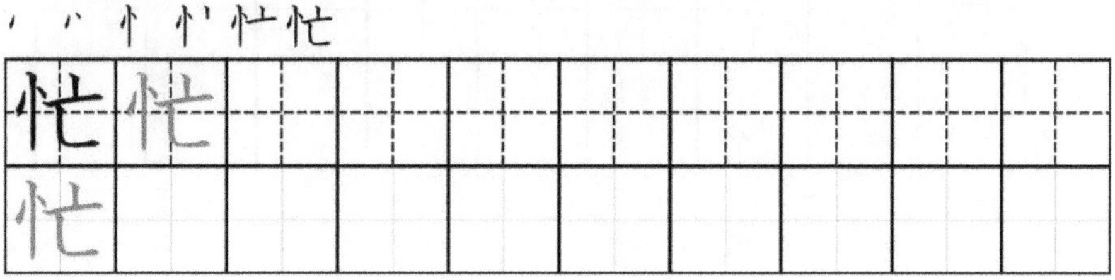

Appendix A

#63 ノ ク タ 夕 多 多

多 多
多

#64 亅 小 小 少

少 少
少

#65 ノ ク 夂

夂 夂
夂

#66 ノ 彳 彳 彳 彳 徍 徍 待 待

待 待
待

#67 丶 亠 亣 立 立 辛 辛 亲 亲 新 新 新 新

新 新
新

#68 ㄑ 女 女 女 妤 好

好 好
好

Appendix A

#69

思 思

思

#70

昨 昨

昨

#71

買 買

買

#72

食 食

食

#73

田 田

田

#74

後 後

後

#75 丿 𠂉 𠂉 午

午 午

午

#76 一 十 土 去 去

去 去

去

#77 丨 冂 日 日 明 明 明 明

明 明

明

#78 丿 人 今 今 今 食 食 食 飲 飲 飲 飲

飲 飲

飲

#79 丿 亻 仁 什 仕

仕 仕

仕

#80 一 一 戸 戸 写 写 写 事

事 事

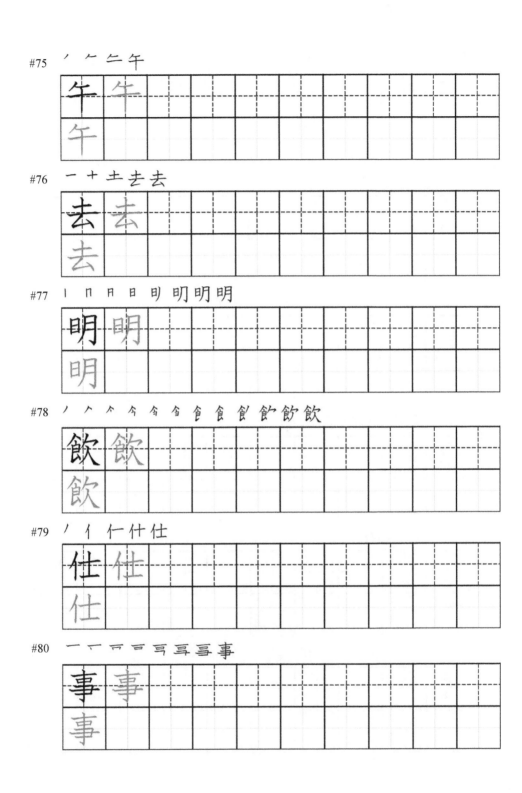

事

#81 ノ ク タ 夕 外

外 外
外

#82 ノ 人 亼 亼 会 会

会 会
会

#83 丶 ラ ネ ネ 礻 社 社

社 社
社

Act 11

#84 一 十 オ 木 木 木 木 木 栏 样 样 様 様 様

様 様
様

#85 丶 亠 亠 言 言 言 言 言 訁 話 話 話 話

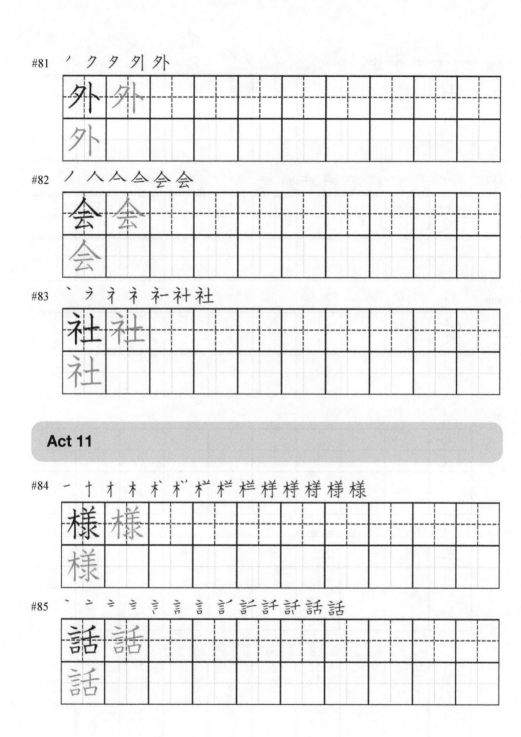

話 話
話

#86 一 十 廾 廿 世

世 世

世

#87 丶 亠 广 广 疒 疒 疒 疒 疲 疲

疲 疲

疲

#88 丿 亻 亻 亻 佢 佢 使 使

使 使

使

#89 丿 亻 亻 亻 竹 作 作

作 作

作

#90 丶 亠 亠 亠 言 言 言

言 言

言

#91 丶 亠 亠 亠 言 言 言 訁 訁 訁 訁 讀 讀 讀

讀 讀

讀

Appendix A

#92 電

電 電
電

#93 京

京 京
京

#94 都

都 都
都

#95 駅

駅 駅
駅

#96 出

出 出
出

#97 東

東 東
東

#98 丨 冂 口

口 口 口

#99 丿 入

入 入 入

#100 一 丆 冂 冂 日 亘 車

車 車 車

#101 丨 冂 日 日 旦 早

早 早 早

#102 丨 冂 冂 冂 同 同

同 同 同

#103 丨 卜 止 止 步 步 步 步

步 步 步

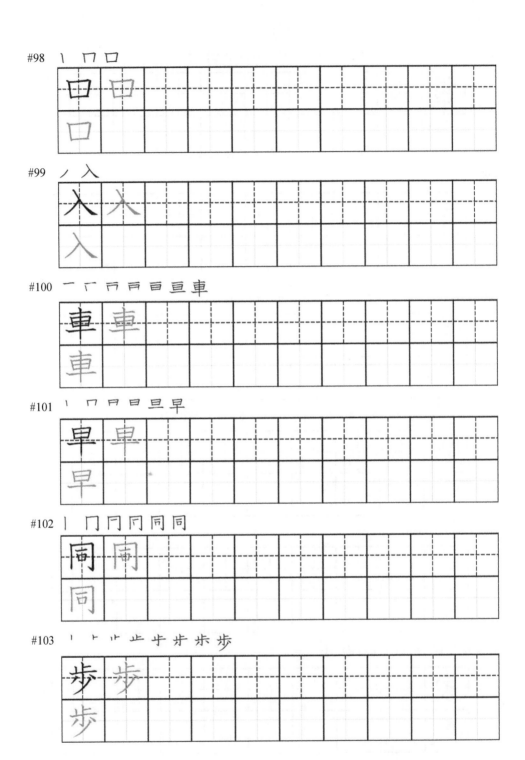

Appendix A

#104
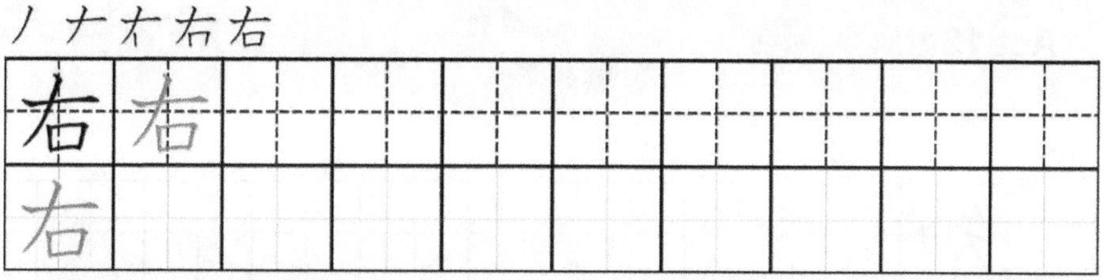

#105
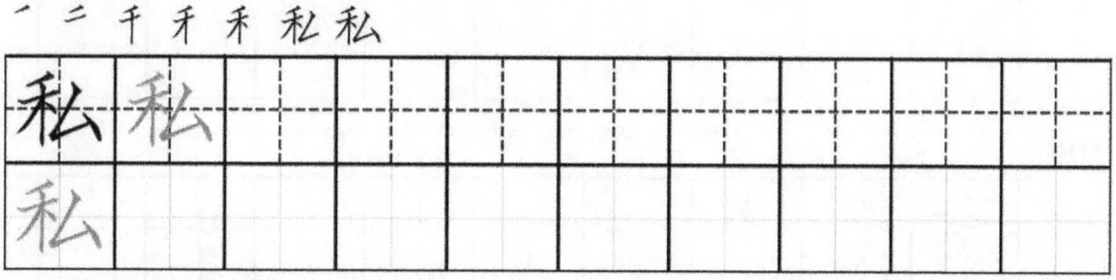

#106
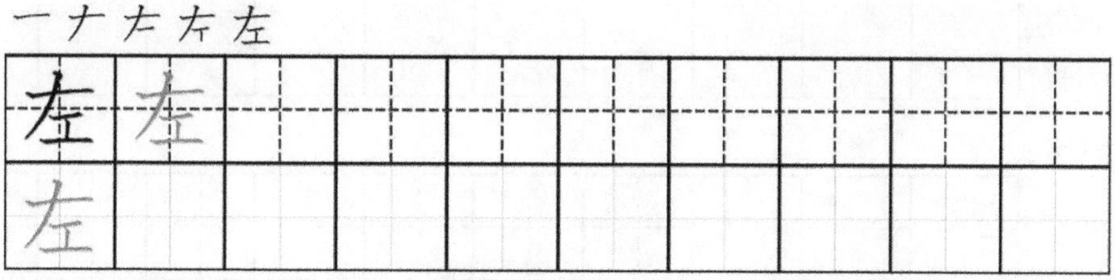

#107
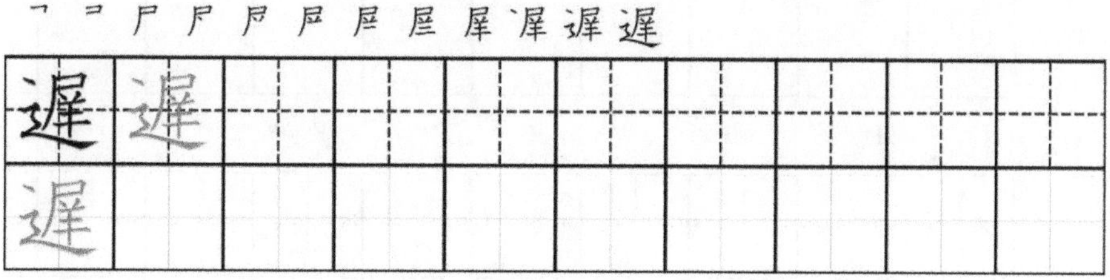

#108
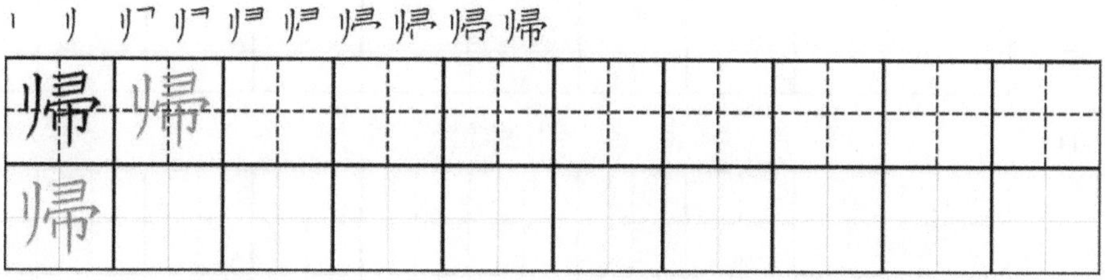

Act 12

#109 知

#110 漢

#111 字

#112 小

#113 教

#114 室

#115 勉

勉 勉

勉

#116 強

強 強

強

#117 弱

弱 弱

弱

#118 天

天 天

天

#119 気

気 気

気

#120 留

留 留

留

#121 短

短 短

短

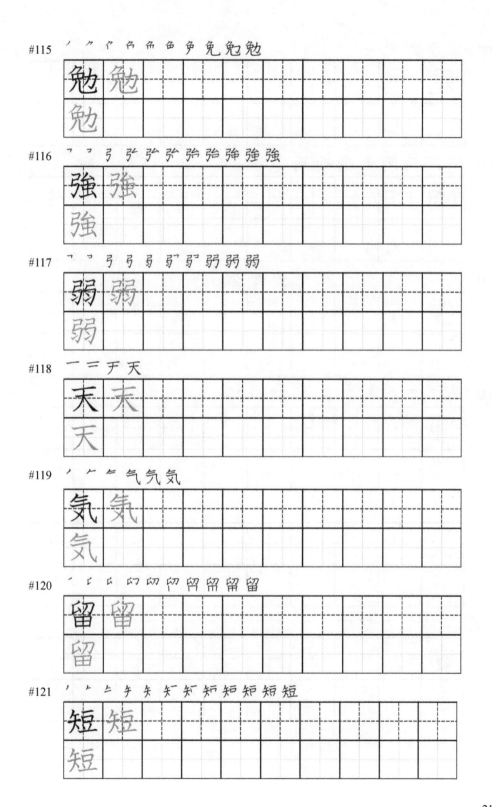

Appendix A

#122 一 二 亍 元

元 元

元

#123 一 厂 冂 帀 帀 雨 雨 雨

雨 雨

雨

#124 一 厂 冖 帀 帀 雨 雨 雨 雪 雪 雪

雪 雪

雪

#125 丶 亠 亠 立 立 产 音 音 音 部 部

部 部

部

#126 丨 厂 F E 巨 镸 镸 長

長 長

長

#127 丶 丷 宀 安 安 安

安 安

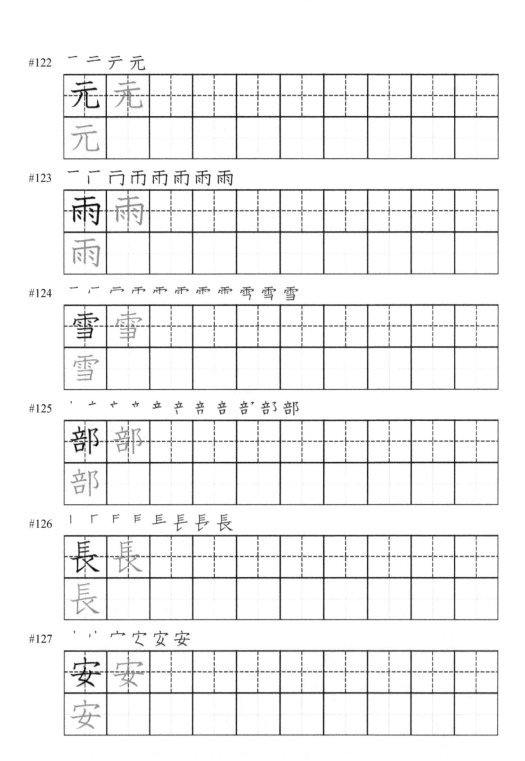

安

#128 ノ 亻 仁 什 休 休

休	休									
休										

#129 丨 冂 日 日 日' 日" 旷 晗 晗 晗 晚 晩

晩	晩									
晩										

#130 ノ 𠆢 亽 今 今 㒳 食 食 飠 飦 飯 飯

飯	飯									
飯										

#131 一 十 艹 古 古 吉 直 卓 卓 朝 朝 朝

朝	朝									
朝										

#132 ㇖ コ 尸 尺 尺 居 昼 昼 昼

昼	昼									
昼										

#133 ノ 𠂉 𠂉 毎 毎 毎

毎	毎									
毎										

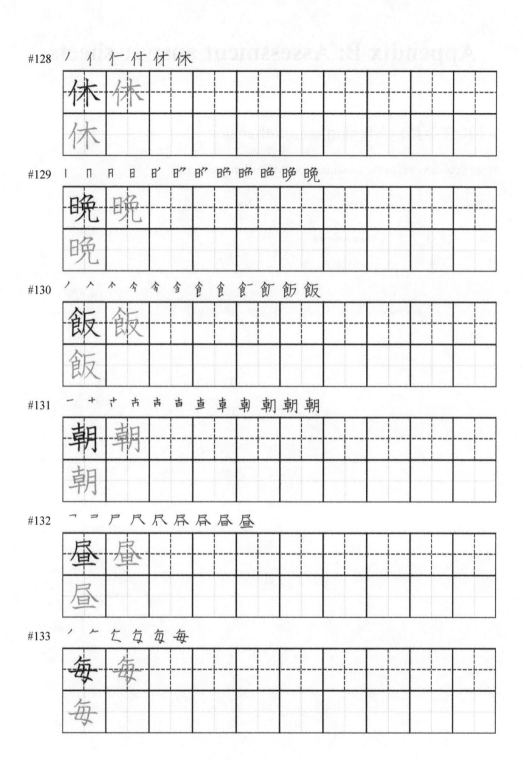

Appendix A

Appendix B: Assessment answer sheets

聞いてみよう Listening comprehension

Write your answers to the Listening comprehension questions.

ACT # __________ Date: ___________ Name: ______________________________

No.	Q	Your Answer
1	a	

読んでみよう Contextualized reading

Write your answers to the Contextualized reading questions.

ACT # __________ Date: ___________ Name: ______________________________

No.	Q	Your Answer
1	a	

Appendix B

書き取り Dictation

Write what you hear.

ACT # __________ Date: ___________ Name: ______________________________

No.	Your Answer
1	

書(か)いてみよう Contextualized writing

Write your responses to the Contextualized writing items.

ACT # __________ Date: ___________ Name: ______________________________

知(し)ってる? What do you know?

Write your answers to the What do you know? questions.

ACT # __________ Date: ___________ Name: ______________________________

1		11		21	
2		12		22	
3		13		23	
4		14		24	
5		15		25	
6		16		26	
7		17		27	
8		18		28	
9		19		29	
10		20		30	

Appendix C: 形(かたち)にスポットライト！ Spotlight on form! Act 7

Act 7: -RU/U Verbs and negative forms (BTS 1)

Here is a table of all Verbs you have learned so far in their citation forms. Fill in the blank cells with the accurate 〜ます form to complete the table. Use hiragana.

-RU Verbs:

citation forms	English	〜ます form
できる	can do	できます
いる	be, exist (animate)	い__________
始(はじ)める	begin something	始(はじ)め__________
食(た)べる	eat	食(た)べ__________
見(み)る	see	見(み)__________
考(かんが)える	think	考(かんが)え__________
決(き)める	decide	決(き)め__________
借(か)りる	borrow	借(か)り__________
いただける	can receive	いただけ__________
任(まか)せる	leave it to someone else	任(まか)せ__________
出(で)る	go out	出(で)__________
教(おし)える	teach	教(おし)え__________
見(み)せる	show	見(み)せ__________
見(み)える	appear	見(み)え__________
存(ぞん)じる	know	存(ぞん)じ__________
勧(すす)める	recommend	勧(すす)め__________
慣(な)れる	get used to	慣(な)れ__________

-U Verbs:

citation forms	English	～ます form
待(ま)つ	wait	待(ま)ちます
持(も)つ	hold	持(も)________
立(た)つ	stand	立(た)________
わかる	understand	わかります
頑張(がんば)る	do one's best	頑張(がんば)________
終(お)わる	end something	終(お)わ________
ある	exist (inanimate)	あ________
帰(かえ)る	return (home)	帰(かえ)________
作(つく)る	make	作(つく)________
取(と)る	take	取(と)________
乗(の)る	ride, get onboard	乗(の)________
かかる	take (time/money)	かか________
要(い)る	need	要(い)________
やる	do	や________
助(たす)かる	be helped	助(たす)か________
参(まい)る	go, come (humble)	参(まい)________
なる	become	な________
撮(と)る	take (a photo)	撮(と)________
座(すわ)る	sit	座(すわ)________
寄(よ)る	drop by	寄(よ)________
おる	be (humble)	お________
困(こま)る	be troubled	困(こま)________
知(し)る	know	知(し)________
言(い)う	is called, say	言(い) います
会(あ)う	see, meet	会(あ)________
違(ちが)う	different from	違(ちが)________
買(か)う	buy	買(か)________
使(つか)う	use	使(つか)________
手(て) 伝(つだ)う	help	手伝(てつだ)________
構(かま)う	mind, care	構(かま)________
伺(うかが)う	visit (humble)	伺(うかが)________
迷(まよ)う	become confused, lost	迷(まよ)________
行(い)く	go	行(い)きます

書く	write	書_________
いただく	eat; receive (humble)	いただ_________
聞く	hear; listen	聞_________
歩く	walk	歩_________
空く	become free	空_________
急ぐ	hurry	急ぎます
呼ぶ	call, invite	呼びます
喜ぶ	be delighted	喜_________
飲む	drink	飲みます
読む	read	読_________
休む	take a break	休_________
頼む	request	頼_________
死ぬ	die	死にます
話す	talk	話します
出す	submit, take out	出_________
申す	say (humble)	申_________

-ARU Verbs:

citation forms	English	～ますform
ござる	have, exist (polite) come, go (honorific)	ございます
いらっしゃる	be (honorific form of いる)	いらっしゃ_________
おっしゃる	say (honorific)	おっしゃ_________

Irregular Verbs

citation forms	English	～ますform
来る	come	来ます
する	do	します

Here is a table of verbs that have not yet been covered. Practice deriving ～ます forms from citation forms by filling in the blank cells, based on the information you are given. Use hiragana.

citation forms	English	～ますform
泳ぐ (-U)	swim (7-2)	泳_________
なさる (-ARU)	do (honorific) (7-4)	なさ_________
寝る (-RU)	sleep (8-1)	寝_________

当たる (-U)	hit on target (8-1)	当た________
謝る (-U)	apologize (9-1)	謝________
遊ぶ (-U)	play (9-3)	遊________
歌う (-U)	sing (9-5)	歌________
入る (-U)	go in (9-6)	入________
続ける (-RU)	continue (10-6)	続け________
承知する	consent (11-1)	承知________
履く (-U)	pull on (11-2)	履________
痛む (-U)	become painful (11-5)	痛________
打つ (-U)	hit (11-6)	打________
足りる (-RU)	be enough (12-3)	足り________
生やす (-U)	grow (12-5)	生や________

Act 7: 〜ない and 〜た forms (BTS 7, 8)

Here is a table of all Verbs you have learned so far in their citation forms. Fill in the blank cells with the accurate 〜ない and 〜た (i.e., informal affirmative past) forms to complete the table. Use hiragana.

-RU Verbs:

citation forms	English	〜ない forms	〜た forms
できる	can do	できない	できた
いる	be, exist (animate)	い________	い________
始める	begin something	始め________	始め________
食べる	eat	食べ________	食べ________
見る	see	見________	見________
考える	think	考え________	考え________
決める	decide	決め________	決め________
借りる	borrow	借り________	借り________
いただける	can receive	いただけ________	いただけ________
任せる	leave it to someone else	任せ________	任せ________
出る	go out	出________	出________
教える	teach	教え________	教え________
見せる	show	見せ________	見せ________
見える	appear	見え________	見え________
存じる	know	存じ________	存じ________

		勧め__________	勧め__________
勧める・薦める	recommend	薦め__________	薦め__________
慣れる	get used to	慣れ__________	慣れ__________
遅れる	run late	遅れ__________	遅れ__________

-U Verbs:

citation forms	English	～ない forms	～た forms
待つ	wait	待たない	待った
持つ	hold	持__________	持__________
立つ	stand	立__________	立__________
わかる	understand	わからない	わかった
頑張る	do one's best	頑張__________	頑張__________
終わる	end something	終わ__________	終わ__________
ある	exist (inanimate)	ない	あ__________
帰る	return (home)	帰__________	帰__________
作る	make	作__________	作__________
取る	take	取__________	取__________
乗る	ride, get onboard	乗__________	乗__________
かかる	take (time/money)	かか__________	かか__________
要る	need	要__________	要__________
やる	do	や__________	や__________
助かる	be helped	助か__________	助か__________
参る	go, come (humble)	参__________	参__________
なる	become	な__________	な__________
撮る	take (a photo)	撮__________	撮__________
座る	sit	座__________	座__________
寄る	drop by	寄__________	寄__________
困る	be troubled	困__________	困__________
知る	know	知__________	知__________
登る	climb	登__________	登__________
下る	go down from	下__________	下__________
走る	run	走__________	走__________
言う	is called, say	言 わない	言った
会う	see, meet	会__________	会__________
違う	different from	違__________	違__________
買う	buy	買__________	買__________

使(つか)う	use	使(つか)______	使(つか)______
手伝(てつだ)う	help	手伝(てつだ)______	手伝(てつだ)______
構(かま)う	mind, care	構(かま)______	構(かま)______
伺(うかが)う	visit (humble)	伺(うかが)______	伺(うかが)______
迷(まよ)う	become confused, lost	迷(まよ)______	迷(まよ)______
書(か)く	write	書(か)かない	書(か)いた
行(い)く	go	行(い)______	行(い)った
いただく	eat; receive (humble)	いただ______	いただ______
聞(き)く	hear; listen	聞(き)______	聞(き)______
歩(ある)く	walk	歩(ある)______	歩(ある)______
空(あ)く	become free	空(あ)______	空(あ)______
急(いそ)ぐ	hurry	急(いそ)がない	急(いそ)いだ
泳(およ)ぐ	swim	泳(およ)______	泳(およ)______
呼(よ)ぶ	call, invite	呼(よ)ばない	呼(よ)んだ
喜(よろこ)ぶ	be delighted	喜(よろこ)______	喜(よろこ)______
飲(の)む	drink	飲(の)まない	飲(の)んだ
読(よ)む	read	読(よ)______	読(よ)______
休(やす)む	take a break	休(やす)______	休(やす)______
頼(たの)む	request	頼(たの)______	頼(たの)______
死(し)ぬ	die	死(し)なない	死(し)んだ
話(はな)す	talk	話(はな)さない	話(はな)した
出(だ)す	submit, take out	出(だ)______	出(だ)______
申(もう)す	say (humble)	申(もう)______	申(もう)______

-ARU Verbs:

citation forms	English	～ない forms	～た forms
いらっしゃる	come, go (honorific), be (honorific form of いる)	いらっしゃらない	いらっしゃった
おっしゃる	say (honorific)	おっしゃ______	おっしゃ______

IRR Verbs

citation forms	English	～ない forms	～た forms
来(く)る	come	来(こ)ない	た
する	do	しない	した

Here is a table of Verbs that have not yet been covered. Practice deriving ～ます forms from citation forms by filling in the blank cells, based on the information you are given. Use hiragana.

citation forms	English	～ます forms
なさる (-ARU)	do (honorific) (7-4)	なさ________
寝(ね)る (-RU)	sleep (8-1)	寝(ね)________
当(あ)たる (-U)	hit on target (8-1)	当(あ)た________
謝(あやま)る (-U)	apologize (9-1)	謝(あやま)________
遊(あそ)ぶ (-U)	play (9-3)	遊(あそ)________
歌(うた)う (-U)	sing (9-5)	歌(うた)________
入(はい)る (-U)	go in (9-6)	入(はい)________
続(つづ)ける (-RU)	continue (10-6)	続(つづ)け________
承知(しょうち)する	consent (11-1)	承知(しょうち)________
履(は)く (-U)	pull on (11-2)	履(は)________
痛(いた)む (-U)	become painful (11-5)	痛(いた)________
打(う)つ (-U)	hit (11-6)	打(う)________
足(た)りる (-RU)	be enough (12-3)	足(た)り________
生(は)やす (-U)	grow (12-5)	生(は)や________

Appendix D: Answer keys

Act 7

7-1-1C Which one is better?

3. d, next week; 4. g, this one; 5. c, tomorrow; 6. i, this year; 7. b, that other place; 8. j, Dad

7-2-1C What's going on?

2-1. c; 2-2. d; 3-1. f; 3-2. e; 4-1. g; 4-2. h; 5-1. j; 5-2. i

7-3-1C Hearsay or not? (BTS 9)

3. hearsay; 4. hearsay; 5. not hearsay; 6. hearsay; 7. not hearsay; 8. not hearsay; 9. hearsay; 10. not hearsay

7-4-1C Agree or disagree?

3. Agree; 4. Dis agree; 5. Agree; 6. Dis agree; 7. Agree; 8. Dis agree

7-5-1C Identifying sentence modifiers

3. don't know-kanji; 4. have-person; 5. swim-time; 6. hurry-job; 7. bring-person

7-6-1C What's going on?

3. b; 4. a; 5. a; 6. b; 7. a; 8. b; 9. b; 10. a; 11. b; 12. a; 13. b

7-6-2C What's going on?

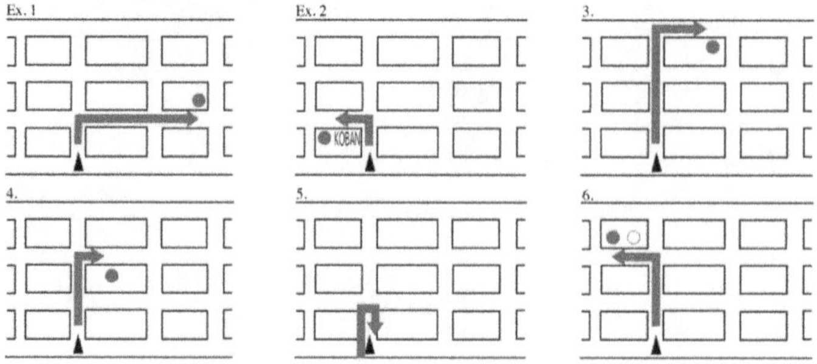

7-7-1R Comparing two items
3. temperature; 4. skill; 5. taste

7-7-2R Expressing surprises
3. b; 4. c; 5. f; 6. a

7-8-1R Coming or going?
3. e; 4. d; 5. f; 6. h; 7. b; 8. c

7-8-2R Guessing what question is being answered
3. 9月のパーティーは何日ですか; 4. ニューヨークは何日からですか; 5. 1日はだれが行きますか; 6. ジョーンズさんもスミスさんも来ますか; 7. ヴェニスにはもう行きましたか; 8. カンファレンスは2月ですか。

7-8-3W Getting information
3. ミーティングは2日ですね。; 4. カンファレンスは3月9日ですね。; 5. パーティーは来月ですね。; 6. 来月はジョーンズさんが行きますね。; 7. 13日はスミスさんが来ませんでしたね。

7-9-2R Which time word is missing?
3. c; 4. d; 5. e; 6. f

7-9-3W Getting information
3. 半月; 4. 半日; 5. 半月; 6. 半時間

聞いてみよう Listening comprehension

1. a. they are really delicious; b. that Yoko is on a diet; c. Yoko is on a diet; last week; d. not to have dessert; to have dessert; 2. a. it's tough; b. that she's used to it; they serve dinner; c. that it's always the same bento; 3. a. to rest a bit; b. there are others who aren't used to it; c. it's a narrow, crowded path; d. since they are at a high altitude, they may feel queasy; e. how much longer they have to go; f. a bit more than an hour; 4. a. it's snowing; not very severe; b. that it would get a bit bad; that it would snow; c. because of the high altitude; 5. a. that it was very sad; b. it was somber; 6. a. when times are tough, a dark room can be more soothing than a bright one; b. the friend's younger sister told him that she read it on the internet; c. that it was on the internet and that his younger sister told him; d. that his younger sister told him; 7. a. the cafeteria where they are now; it's convenient and the specials are delicious; b. he wants to eat at a quieter place; c. the cafeteria, because they don't have much time before their next class; d. because Brian would like something hot.

読んでみよう Contextualized reading

(1) a. two; b. Wilmington; c. Wendy Martin (San Diego, California) and Andrew Jones (San Jose, California); d. Jennifer Williams (Madison, Wisconsin)
(2) a. To go to karaoke with Martin-san now; b. Karaoke until about 10:30.
(3) a. For coming to the club the other day; b. To come to class again next month on the 5th (Mon.) at 9:00.
(4) a. a waiting list; b. Yamada; c. Hartford. d. Sheffer at 7:30; 4. Kanda and Yoshimoto

書き取り Dictation

1. 来月はカリフォルニアに行くからちょっと……。
2. マーティンさんがまだ来ないんです。
3. チェックインは何時だって?
4. 来テーィ月一の、パがすで行くいらっしゃいますか。
5. ベートヴェンよりモーツァルトのほうがいい。
6. 2月18日じゃなくて19日だよ。
7. ヴァイオリンはしないとおっしゃっていました。
8. 1時半から3時半までなんですか。

書いてみよう Contextualized writing

1. ジェシカ、この間はおいしいランチどうもありがとう。
2. フォードさん、あさってのミーティング、3時じゃなくて3時半からじゃないですか。
3. ヴィヴィアン、来月10日(月)の19時から21時半ごろまでみんなでカラオケに行くんだけど、ヴィヴィアンもよかったら来ない?

知ってる? What do you know?

1	C	11	B	21	A	31	B
2	B	12	A	22	B	32	C
3	B	13	C	23	A	33	A
4	A	14	C	24	B	34	A
5	A	15	B	25	C	35	B
6	C	16	B	26	A		
7	B	17	A	27	B		
8	A	18	C	28	C		
9	C	19	B	29	C		
10	A	20	A	30	B		

Act 8

8-1-1C What's happening?
3. b; 4. d; 5. c; 6. f; 7. a; 8. g

8-1-2C I do it every…
3. g; 4. d; 5. h; 6. a; 7. c; 8. e

8-2-1C Affirmative and negative requests
3. d, affirmative; 4. e, negative; 5. h, affirmative; 6. c, negative; 7. a, negative; 8. g, affirmative; 9. j, negative

8-2-2C Giving reasons
3. c; 4. b; 5. b; 6. a; 7. c; 8. a; 9. c; 10. b; 11. a

8-3-1C Invitation to do what?
3. sit; 4. be comfortable; 5. drink tea; 6. don't hold back; 7. sleep; 8. use an extra blanket; 9. have breakfast; 10. use a towel; 11. come again; 12. take care

8-4-1C How often?
3. c; 4. f; 5. a; 6. b

8-5-2C What's about to happen?
3. become lost; 4. become hungry; 5. be able to talk; 6. become thirsty; 7. wake up; 8. clear up; 9. cry; 10. begin

8-6-1C How often does this happen?
3. once in a while; 4. every year; 5. frequently; 6. always; 7. without failure

8-6-2C How many?
3. four tests, more; 4. one person, less; 5. one time, less; 6. ten posters, more; 7. two hours, less; 8. three times, more; 9. one cake, less

8-7-1R Identifying dates and times
3. June 7th and August 2nd; 4. Monday at 8:30; 5. 1986, May 20th

8-7-3W Writing down prices

四九〇円
五二〇円
六一〇円
六七〇円

8-8-1R Reacting with an appropriate *aizuchi*
3. へえ; 4. たしかに; 5. ふうん; そうだね; なるほど; やっぱり

8-8-3W What language is it?
3. インドネシア語; ベトナム語; ロシア語; ドイツ語; イタリア語

8-9-1R Greetings
3. h; 4. d; 5. e; 6. g; 7. c; 8. i; 9. a

8-9-3W Writing a guest list
フランス人の大学生　3人; 日本語の先生　5人; インターンの学生　12人

聞いてみよう Listening comprehension

1. a. the weather has cleared up; b. he thought it would be a bit dangerous since it's gotten dark and it looked like it would rain; 2. a. he wakes up; b. she sleeps until 10:00; c. he sleeps until late too; 3. a. she got married; b. for congratulating her on her wedding; c. very nice, but sometimes he says harsh things; 4. a. the number of vacation days annually; b. 20 days per year; most people take six or seven days off in both winter and summer, and many take the rest in May; 5. a. Suzuki-san has been there two or three times on business; b. winter; 6. a. a strange noise; b. it's not unpleasant, not common, and not made by a person; 7. a. in the room upstairs; b. what is Kawakami-san's first name?; c. he can't remember; 8. a. *rikon*; divorce; b. his mother lives in Oregon; his father is in New York; 9. a. whether he's interrupting something; b. she says that they just finished so he's not interrupting at all; 10. a. that it's new; b. it hasn't been used even once; c. she'll bring it on Monday; 11. a. a client; b. a complaint; c. he's griped about various matters many times in the past; d. he didn't look like a person who would be a nuisance; 12. a. to consult with the division chief; b. that she not say anything to the client right away, that he speak with the client first.

読んでみよう Contextualized reading

(1) a. for visiting him/her the other day; b. a souvenir; c. (3)
(2) a. next month's tour; b. 95,000 yen; expensive; c. Eri hasn't been to one but she heard that it's a very good tour; Wow, pretty! Sasha wants to go.
(3) a. globalization and Japanese; b. Steve Johnson (Harvard University); c. February 6th (M), lecture from 4:30 to 5:30 and Q & A session from 5:30 to 6:00; Friend Hall; d. refreshments

書き取り Dictation

1. よろしくお願いします。
2. そんなによさそうな大学じゃないね。
3. あさっては先生がいらっしゃいません。
4. 日本語は今年で二年目になります。
5. 一人四万五千円ぐらいだろう。
6. メキシコに行ったことありますか?
7. 今は何もしないでください。
8. 今日こっちに来てみる?

書いてみよう Contextualized writing

1. リー先生、おめでとうございます!

2.
先日はおみやげありがとうございました。これ、つまらないものですが、どうぞ。これからもよろしくお願いします。

3.
「日本のインターンシッププログラム」
ゲストスピーカー:カレン・カラハン先生
日時:3月8日(月)

- 9時半〜10時半　レクチャー
- 10時半〜11時半　パネルディスカッション

場所:ユニオンビルディング　セミナールームC
ランチもあります。どうぞ来てください!

知ってる? What do you know?

1	B	11	B	21	A
2	B	12	B	22	C
3	C	13	A	23	
4	B	14	B	24	

5	A	15	A	25	
6	C	16	A	26	
7	B	17	C	27	
8	C	18	A	28	
9	B	19	B	29	
10	A	20	C	30	

Act 9

9-1-1C Identifying sentence modifiers

3. a computer, Yuya-kun was using until late yesterday; 4. ramen, Brian says is inexpensive and delicious; 5. A report, Kanda-san and Sasha wrote together; 6. university, Ishikawa-kun has been attending since last semester; 7. intern, Terada-san said is rude and disagreeable; 8. Cook-san, said that he loves Japan

9-2-2C Confirming something

3. c; 4. b; 5. b; 6. c; 7. d; 8. a; 9. d; 10. c; 11. b; 12. a

9-2-1C What's the amount?

3. 1/25, size; 4. 27.8, temperature; 5. 1/2, people; 6. 0.45, weight; 7. 1/4, homework

9-2-2C For what purpose?

3. b; 4. f; 5. d; 6. e

9-3-1C What job?

3. office job; 4. company employee; 5. lawyer; 6. freelance job; 7. something law related; 8. engineer

9-4-1C Where's the city?

3. g; 4. d; 5. a; 6. b; 7. f

9-4-2C Which is the most...

3. fastest, taxi; 4. hottest, August; 5. strongest, Noguchi-san; 6. biggest, Sapporo; 7. cheapest, supermarket

9-5-1C Hobbies

3. Omura-san, kendo; 4. Tomoda-san, taking pictures; 5. Yui-chan, cooking; 6. Takahashi-san, watching soccer games; 7. Uchida-san, listening to music and reading books; 8. Hiroshi-kun, drawing pictures

9-7-1R Discussing schedules

3. Wednesday is no good; 4. Friday is better than Thursday; 5. They both said Saturday and Sunday are good.

9-6-1C Order of events

3. 1, 2; 4. 2, 1; 5. 1, 2; 6. 1, 2

9-6-2C Multiplication

3. yakitori, three, fifteen; 4. clients/customers, two, twenty; 5. people/servings, ten, forty; 6. books, five, fifty

9-7-1R Discussing schedules

3. Wednesday is no good; 4. Friday is better than Thursday; 5. They both said Saturday and Sunday are good.

9-7-2R Guessing whether it's a yes or no

3. N; 4. Y; 5. N; 6. Y

9-7-3W Which day is it?

3. 木曜日; 4. 来週の土日; 5. 来週の水曜日から土曜日まで

9-8-1R Discussing duration and height

3. thirty minutes; 4. five minutes; 5. one to two minutes; 6. 147 meters; 7. twelve hours and thirty minutes; 8. 300 meters

9-8-2R Discussing occupations

3. American high school; 4. Kawakami-san; 5. two-thirds of them are boys and one third of them are girls

9-8-3W Identifying names of people, high schools, and colleges

3. 高校の名前; 4. 大学の名前; 5. 人の名前; 6. 高校の名前; 7. 大学の名前; 9. 人の名前

9-8-4W Writing time duration

3. 4 時間 45 分; 4.12、3 分; 5. 78 時間 50 分; 6. 2 時間 40 分

9-9-1R Introduction

3. Yamamoto from JLC; 4. Li from China; 5. Murakami from Shikoku University; 6. Yamanaka from Portland State University; 7. Kawashita from Science Club

9-9-2R Identifying the one

Amy – E; Eddy – N/A; Emily – G; Kathy – C; Kimberly – K; James – N/A; Jeremiah – A; Josh – N/A; Wilson – F; Williams – I

9-9-3R Discussing plans

3. after asking Kawamura-sensei; 4. after Yamashita-san comes; 5. next week; 6. after finding out the schedule; 7. after becoming an adult; 8. after becoming a high school teacher

9-9-4W Writing down names

3. 九州大学、立川; 4. ユタ州立大学、木下; 5. シンガポール国立大学、川中; 6. ニューヨーク大学、村上

聞いてみよう Listening comprehension

1. a. who made the design; b. the colors; c. that even if he spent ten times the amount of time, he wouldn't be able to create such a design; 2. a. they threw quite a lot away; b. about three-fifths done; c. they still have the room upstairs to clean; d. they don't have to clean the upstairs room; 3. a. for the success of the project; b. eat and drink; 4. a. because he didn't tell his wife that he'd go out drinking with his office colleagues; b. go ahead and have dinner without him; 5. a. she's given it a lot of thought, but she hasn't begun to write it; b. that she won't have it finished by the day after tomorrow; c. why is she so unconcerned?; 6. a. how quickly she wrote the report; b. that it took him five times as long to write his report; c. he's not very good at writing in English; 7. a. research institute; b. he analyzes architectural designs; c. design buildings; 8. a. Sapporo, Sendai, Kanazawa; b. he moved often because of his father's work; c. his younger sister liked Kanazawa the best; d. why he liked it; 9. a. kendo; b. they both don't want to quit because when they are practicing they can forget all about their work; c. he sometimes has to go away for business on his practice day; d. he says it's too bad but 'work is work'; 10. a. her cell phone; b. the living room and the kitchen; c. because she had just taken a shower; d. that she often forgets where she puts her phone.

読んでみよう Contextualized reading

(1) Part 1. a. Dr. Kawamura from Kyushu University; b. Thursday from 2:30 p.m. to 4:00 p.m. at Lincoln Hall 201; c. Business Japanese: Communication Manners; Part 2. a. Dr. Yamashita from Shikoku University; b. Friday from 9:00 a.m. to 10:45 a.m. at Friend Hall 180; c. internship: Japanese and globalization

(2) a. Kinoshita; b. next Tuesday by Dr. Jones from Singapore National University; c. an invitation about the dinner session at 6:00 p.m. at a place called Sun Flower on Monday (the day before the lecture); d. whether I understand Chinese because Chinese menus are also available

書き取り Dictation

1. 中国語が分かるのは川村さんです。
2. ちょっと聞きに行ってきます。
3. 先生に聞いてから行きましょう。
4. 水曜日でも木曜日でもいいですよ。

5. 来週の金曜日とか土曜日とかはどう？
6. だって分からないし、つまらないんだもん。
7. オハイオ州立大学に行ってみたいなぁ。
8. どうして高校の先生になりたいんですか？

書いてみよう Contextualized writing

1. ちょっと中村先生に今週の金曜日のスケジュールを聞きに行って来ます。
2. 1月17日（来週の木曜日）のレクチャーは12時45分からになりました。
3. 来週の水曜日にポートランド州立大学の川上先生のレクチャーがあります。前日の火曜日の17時15分からワークショップもあるのですが、よかったら来ませんか？

知ってる? What do you know?

1	C	11	A	21	B
2	A	12	B	22	C
3	A	13	B	23	A
4	A	14	C	24	A
5	B	15	B	25	
6	A	16	C	26	
7	C	17	C	27	
8	B	18	B	28	
9	C	19	A	29	
10	B	20	C	30	

Act 10

10-1-1C Doing what in advance?
3. n; 4. none; 5. h; 6. none; 7. i; 8. e

10-1-2C What activities are suggested?
3. h; 4. e; 5. a; 6. c; 7. i; 8. b; 9. f; 10. g

10-2-1C In the middle of…
3. a; 4. c; 5. a; 6. b; 7. b; 8. c

10-2-2C I'm so sorry

3. a, b, d; 4. a, b; 5. a, b, d; 6. a, b; 7. a.; 8. a, b, d

10-3-1C What's going on?

3. e; 4. b; 5. d; 6. c

10-3-2C What did they order?

3. Fish combo; 4. Tempura udon; 5. Orange juice; 6. The same item as what the people at the next table are eating; 7. Tempura combo; 8. Meat combo with soup and rice

10-4-1C How certain?

3. b; 4. a; 5. c; 6. a; 7. b; 8. c

10-5-1C How is self-image restored?

3. many errors during interpretation/research more in advance; 4. too much time spent on the experiment/prepare better; 5. report being late/submit it sooner; 6. awkward question during a meeting/consider the question content more; 7. reservation made for the wrong time/check the information carefully

10-6-1C What is being described?

3. what he is good at in school/foreign languages; 4. dream after graduation/walk through countries of the world by himself alone; 5. what he always does before his Spanish class/listen to Spanish songs; 6. what he often does during summer breaks/part-time job, usually, but occasionally, a two or three day trip with his family; 7. what he does before an exam/review, of course, but relaxation is also important.

10-6-2C Who has more?

3. worse Japanese score, the speaker; 4. better at golf, this year; 5. colder, last week; 6. better at aikido, this month; 7. knows more foreign languages, Yamazaki-san

10-7-1R Doing things ahead of time

3. arrive by 10:30, a new teacher is coming on Friday, explanatory; 4. go to the restroom ahead of time, there will be more people from three o'clock, explanatory; 5. look at the list during this week, next week appears to get busy, direct cause

10-7-2R What does he suggest?

3. write about last week on newspaper; 4. try going to that new restaurant; 5. ask Eiko-san as well; 6. write emails in English sometimes

10-7-3W Describing recipes
火：見たことのないレシピ; 水：待たなくてもすぐできるレシピ; 木：忙しくてもすぐできるレシピ; 金：ビタミンCの多いレシピ; 土：カロリーが少ないレシピ

10-8-1R Who is being more polite?
3. ウェイター（お待ちください；お待たせいたしました；Xでございます）; 4. 田中&山上（Xでいらっしゃいます；Xでございます；いたします）; 5. バーテンダー（Xでございます；かしこまりました）; 6. ミラー（よろしければ；～てくださいません）; 7. 学生（もうしわけありませんでした）; 8. デボラ（お分かり）

10-8-2R Is Sasha certain?
4. skeptical; 5. certain; 6. tentative; 7. certain

10-8-3W Writing reminders on a note
3. スポーツが好きな, 川上さん; 4. ジャイアンツのゲームを見に行った, 去年; 5. コーラ飲む, 田中さんと田村さん; 6. 午前中がいいと思っている, 金田さんだけ

10-9-1R Expectation vs. reality
3. there are fewer people on business than expected; 4. there aren't as many people going outside of the country as expected; 5. this year's Japanese Language Club is better than last year's; 6. Aida-san's smartphone is not as new; 7. (someone) likes sociology better than business; 8. university students aren't as busy

10-9-2R Receiving words of advice
3. 会社; 4. 大学; 5. 会社; 6. 大学; 7. 大学

10-9-3W Jotting down a schedule

	午前中	午後
月	Ex. 1. 大学	仕事
火	大学	仕事
水	大学	仕事
木	買いもの	仕事
金	Ex. 2. ネットワークビジネス会社	仕事
土	ジム	外食
日	ジム	外食

聞いてみよう Listening comprehension

1. a. the team didn't get as many points as they expected; b. they had no points until the eighth (inning); 2. a. she is a customer, he is a host; b. how many are in the party?; c. five; d. seats that are best for children; her party will have children; 3. a. the tempura special with a small portion of rice; 4. a. she's disappointed; it's a little salty; b. it's not as sour as she expected; it's not sweet either; 5. a. for interrupting in the middle of her work; b. the event week after next should end by 4:30 p.m.; c. he thought it might be a good idea to ask again beforehand; d. to end at 4:30; 6. a. she came to do research; b. he omitted that her university was a state university; c. he was nervous; d. there's another university that doesn't have 'state' in the name; 7. a. Keiko Smith; b. her mother is Japanese and gave her a Japanese name; c. Japanese is a foreign language for her; d. to interpret (for a business) connected with law; e. specialized/technical vocabulary; f. until the year after next; 8. a. is this a national university? or private?; b. it's prefectural; c. it has new majors in computer (science) and engineering; it has many students from Asia and Africa so the food in the cafeteria is pretty interesting; 9. a. Japanese; b. so-so, below the average score; c. he uses more time for fun than for study; d. he studied all day the day before the exam; e. it's not enough to study the day before; she saw him and he was studying as seriously as he says; f. he's bad at Japanese; g. university is coming soon; 10. a. she's on a business trip; b. she's away on business a lot; c. Kyoto and Matsuyama; d. until the middle of this week; 11. a. he had an interesting dream yesterday; b. singing *enka* on television; c. he's pretty good, but in his dream he was especially good

読んでみよう Contextualized reading

(1) a. Nitta ; b. new/fresh cookies from Sweets Shop; c. yesterday, because Nitta heard that I (the writer) liked these cookies
(2) a. Tamura; b. Tamura tried to write a program in English; there may be some parts that are hard to see; c. to check the English by tomorrow morning
(3) a. whether Kanda-san is busy tomorrow afternoon; Kanda-san isn't as busy as he thought he would be; b. they are going to go out to eat after work at a buffet restaurant that opened last year; c. he is going to skip lunch tomorrow; d. drink together because it's Friday and it's been a while (since the last time); e. the usual place

書き取り Dictation

1. 少々お待ちください。
2. 昨日から忙しくてすみません。
3. 明日の午後までに見ておこう。
4. 思ったほど新しくないとか。
5. 会社で仕事中かもしれません。
6. 去年より外国人が多いので、英語で書こう。
7. お飲みものは何がお好きですか。
8. 田中さんは外食することが多くて……。

書いてみよう Contextualized writing

1.
会社の後、みんなで飲みに行こうよ!

2.
中田さん
昨日はクッキーを買ってきてくださってありがとうございました。これ、ちょっと食べにくいかもしれませんが、思ったよりおいしくできたので、よかったらどうぞ。

3.
田村さん
仕事のプレゼンを日本語でしようと思っているので、ハンドアウトを日本語で書いてみました。お忙しいところすみませんが、明日の午後までに見ておいていただけないでしょうか。
よろしくお願いします。

知ってる? What do you know?

1	B	11	C	21	A
2	A	12	B	22	C
3	C	13	A	23	
4	C	14	C	24	

5	C	15	C	25	
6	A	16	B	26	
7	A	17	B	27	
8	B	18	C	28	
9	B	19	A	29	
10	A	20	B	30	

Act 11

11-1-1C Business phone conversations

2. Name: Fujita, Purpose: b, Time: 16th, 1:00 p.m.; 3. Name: Kikuchi, Purpose: a, Time: the other day; 4. Name: Hara, Purpose: b, Time: 25th, 2:30 p.m.

11-2-1C Meanings of 〜たら + non-past

3. statement; 4. suggestion; 5. statement; 6. suggestion; 7. statement; 8. request; 9. statement

11-3-1C Meanings of 〜ことにする

3. decision; 4. assumption; 5. routine; 6. assumption; 7. decision; 8. routine; 9. assumption

11-3-2C Who are these people?

3. (g) Watanabe-san; 4. (h) Nakamura-san; 5. (b) Yoshida-san; 6. (f) Matsumoto-san; 7. (d) Hayashi-san; 8. (c) Inoue-san

11-4-1C Who is it?

3. uncle (in-group); 4. grandmother (polite); 5. cousin (in-group); 6. grandfather (in-group); 7. grandmother (in-group); 8. cousin (polite); 9. aunt (in-group)

11-4-2C From a literary perspective…

3. social; 4. American; 5. legal; 6. educational; 7. linguistic; 8. practical

11-5-1C Where does it hurt?

3. arm-prickling pain/stinging; 4. stomach-nauseated/queasy; 5. eye-itchy; 6. throat-dry; 7. shoulder-throbbing

11-5-2C Meanings of 〜たら + past

3. uncontrollable; 4. imagined; 5. imagined; 6. uncontrollable; 7. imagined; 8. imagined; 9. uncontrollable; 10. uncontrollable

11-7-1R Filling in if or when statements

3. c. 4. e; 5. d; 6. g; 7. i; 8. h; 9. b

11-7-2R Giving suggestions

3. i; 4. a; 5. f; 6. e; 7. h; 8. b; 9. d

11-7-3W Writing initial greetings in a letter

3. 作ってくださって; 4. お世話; 5. お疲れ様; 6. お電話; 7. 使ってくださって

11-8-1R Making logical decisions

3. not to attend conferences (expensive and your schedule gets busy); 4. not to go to Tokyo (there are too many people and going there costs money); 5. go to Kyoto University (because it is hard to get into even if you want to); 6. come by later because someone was out of office; 8. take the taxi (the train to Kyoto is no longer in service)

11-8-2R Expressing imagined conditions

3. g; 4. f; 5. d; 6. b; 7. c

11-8-3W Writing down important information on a memo

3. 出口; 4. 東大の田口先生; 5. 京都大学; 6. 高校の入り口; 7. 京都のスイーツ; 8. 駅の東口

11-9-1R Finishing a story with a punch line

3. f; 4. b; 5. c; 6. a

11-9-2R Telling a story

3. b > d > c > a; 4. d > a > c > b; 5. c > a > b > d; 6. a > d > b > c

11-9-3W Leaving a memo

3. 早く帰ります; 4. 同じ電車で行ったら; 5. 出たら左; 6. 歩いて帰ります

聞いてみよう Listening comprehension

1. a. sales division; b. Tamura-san; c. two o'clock, Tuesday next week; d. third floor; 2. a. planning division; b. February 20, something is due by then; c. nothing, he has everything; d. he will tell the chief something; 3. a. Takeda, company president; b. she was late/delayed in telling him the location for something; c. it will be at a restaurant called "Europe" on the twenty-seventh floor; 4. a. he got married; b. that's who he married; c. same age; d. she got into graduate school before he did (so she is the *senpai)*; 5. a. she got a job; b. Aoi Publishing; he had an offer from Australia; c. her parents are already seventy and she worries about them; d. she shows "filial

piety" (concern for her parents); 6. a. if she knows what this word means; b. she's never seen it; c. he'll ask Ota-kun; 7. a. everyone overuses computers; b. it depends on the person, it isn't everyone; c. isn't it (true of) everyone here (in this place)?; 8. a. a social problem, not just a school problem; b. it has gotten worse; c. if there isn't a more proactive solution; d. when you consider children's feelings, it isn't simple; e. his heart aches; 9. a. he denies it; b. he says yeah (うん) and right (そう), but he isn't trying to understand; c. he says that's overthinking; d. what she said just now?; if he was listening he'll know; e. no; f. she'll explain one more time so he should listen; she's offended; 10. a. the division chief's hair style; b. it's odd; c. it suits the chief's glasses and positive image; 11. a. it looks easy to use; b. if they clean it up it will be pretty; 12. a. he didn't understand something and was bothered by it; b. he conferred with Prof. Sakamoto, who very kindly explained it; 13. a. she hasn't been able to contact Yagi-san; b. in the hospital; c. he called her home, planning to leave a message because he thought the same thing

読んでみよう Contextualized reading

(1) a. Ukyo from Japan Store; b. a formal relationship; I provide a service for her; c. the same place as last year (the convenience store on the right as I exit out of the East Exit of Kyoto Station); d. call if I can't find her (lit. can't understand the direction).

(2) a. that I worked late; b. cake; Higashi and Yamaguchi made it yesterday; they put maple syrup and it turned out tastier than expected; c. eat it before going home

(3) a. by leaving work one hour early and taking the train and walking because Jones-san said the place doesn't have a space for a car (parking); b. She is upset because she found a newly built space for parking cars; c. He said "that's why you were late!"; He apologizes because he hadn't read the message until now; d. if she had used the car to get there

書き取り Dictation

1. 遅くまでお疲れ様でした。
2. 先日はお世話になりました。
3. 私の電話、使ってみたら?
4. 東京から京都までのバス
5. チーズを入れて作ってみたらおいしくなった。
6. 駅の東口で待っていたら?
7. 今日は歩いて帰ります。
8. この言語は左から右に読みます。

書いてみよう Contextualized writing

1.
左京さん
遅くまでお疲れ様です。明日も同じ仕事が入っていますが、私は少し早めに出ますので、何か分からないことがあったらお電話ください。

2.
山口さん
いつもお世話様です。京都のマップ、駅から歩いていらっしゃると聞いたので、よかったらお使いください。

3.
右京さん
東さんが作ってみてよかったと言ってたレシピの本です。お疲れでなかったら帰りの電車で読んでみてください。

知ってる? What do you know?

1	B	11	B	21	A
2	A	12	A	22	B
3	A	13	A	23	C
4	C	14	C	24	
5	C	15	C	25	
6	B	16	B	26	
7	A	17	B	27	
8	B	18	C	28	
9	A	19	B	29	
10	C	20	C	30	

Act 12

12-1-1C Who benefits?

3. beneficial; 4. not beneficial; 5. beneficial; 6. beneficial; 7. not beneficial; 8. beneficial; 9. not beneficial

12-2-1C Whether or not…

3. whether it is his wife or not; 4. whether it is in English or Japanese; 5. whether it was sent yesterday or the day before; 6. whether it will be this month or not; 7. whether it is above or below average; 8. whether she will come or not; 9. whether it is tasty or not; 10. whether he lives in Tokyo or not

12-3-1C Whether or not…

3. what he said he's bad at; 4. what kind of Japanese food she likes; 5. how many people there are; 6. how many minutes late it will be; 7. what his condition is; 8. when she's going to New York; 9. how long it will take; 10. what the score was; 11. what to do

12-4-1C Who got it?

3. the speaker; 4. Suzuki-san; 5. the speaker; 6. Suzuki-san; 7. Yagi-bucho; 8. the speaker; 9. the speaker; 10. Yagi-bucho

12-4-2C Who did it?

3. the speaker; 4. another person; 5. another person; 6. the speaker; 7. another person; 8. another person; 9. another person

12-4-3C Isn't there a different reason?

3. he ate too much; 4. there's too much stuff; 5. he has too much to do; 6. he hasn't looked at the textbook; 7. it's in his bag

12-5-1C She wants you to do it.

3. Tanaka-san wants someone to do it; 4. someone wants Tanaka-san to do it; 5. Tanaka-san wants someone to do it; 6. Tanaka-san wants someone to do it; 7. someone wants Tanaka-san to do it; 8. Tanaka-san wants someone to do it; 9. someone wants Tanaka-san to do it; 10. someone wants Tanaka-san to do it

12-6-1C What's going on?

3. b; 4. c; 5. a; 6. b; 7. a; 8. a; 9. a

12-7-1R Someone does you a favor

3. b; 4. e; 5. c; 6. f

12-7-2R Making logical assumptions

3. a; 4. c; 5. g; 6. f; 7. b

12-7-3W Making a request with an embedded yes/no question

3. 漢字・どう(漢字じゃない); 4. 教室・どう(教室じゃない); 5. 強いか・どう(弱い); 6. 勉強していい・どう(してよくない)

12-8-1R Verbs of giving and receiving

3. b; 4. c; 5. a; 6. f

12-8-2R Questions with embedded information

3. e; 4. a; 5. f; 6. g; 7. b; 8. c

12-8-3W Greetings

3. 川上先生; 雪の中いらしてくださって; 4. 東コーチ; 短い間; お世話に; 5. 山口様; 留学生をホストしてくださって; 6. 国立様; 雨の天気になってしまいました

12-9-1R Things I would like you to do…

3. h; 4. i; 5. c; 6. b; 7. f; 8. d; 9. e

12-9-2R Shall I volunteer?

3. f; 4. e; 5. c; 6. d; 7. a

12-9-3W Warning with consequences

3. b; 4. d; 5. f; 6. a; 7. g

12-9-4W Rephrasing statements

4. 短いと; 5. 午後からだったら; 6. 少なかったら; 7. 安くて; 8. 下手じゃないと; 9.大人で; 10. 女の人じゃなかったら; 11. 休んで; 12. 昼休みの前だと

聞いてみよう Listening comprehension

1. a. lend his cousin a bag; b. give it to her; c. return it after she uses it; 2. a. what she should do next; b. put this on the shelf in the room next door, and clean up the top of the desk; 3. a. she likes cleaning; b. getting her to clean up the entire kitchen; c. take her home by car; d. she hasn't had enough exercise lately, and he still has things to do; e. keep going; 4. a. she thinks that it is a mascot character from Kumamoto; b. whether she has been there; c. she may have been there as a child, but she doesn't remember clearly; people are kind and the food is delicious; 5. a. he stayed up late reading manga/comics; b. his eyes got weak, and he fell asleep in class from a lack of sleep; c. nine; in third grade; 6. a. long-haired, cute; b. it's smart; c. he doesn't know if it's smart or not; d. which he likes better—dogs or cats; e. he prefers cats; they're obedient/quiet; f. her apartment is small; 7. a. in restaurants they say, "this is a dessert that young women like"; b. if men want the dessert it's hard to order; the same for older women; when young women are spoken to that way, even if they want to eat it they lose their desire for it (they become not wanting to eat); 8. a. he has twin younger sisters; b. they couldn't tell them apart when they

stood next to each other; 9. a. the furniture; b. it has a long history; c. it must be expensive; d. it's not expensive so it's hard to get a reservation 10. a. explain how to use this, to customers; b. he has to get it ready; c. he'll guide them; 11. a. he makes her breakfast; b. he is a morning person and his wife is a night person; 12. a. it's fine for those who are sitting to remain sitting and those who are standing to remain standing; b. move their heads slowly to the right, then to the left

読んでみよう Contextualized reading

(1) a. everyday in the morning; b. she wishes that someone would make breakfast for her sometimes; c. Shall I make it for you?

(2) a. lunch for someone at her company; the person said it was tasty; b. she is going to make it again and says that it would be nice if the person would eat it again; c. Eri asks for whom it was made for and wonders if the person is "the one."

(3) a. make dinner; b. she won't have time to make dinner if she doesn't leave soon; c. probably her coworker because she thanks her for working late and talks about work tomorrow.

書き取り Dictation

1. 晩ご飯に天ぷら作ってくれてありがとう。
2. 部長、短い間でしたがお世話になりました。
3. 今は雨弱いけど、昼になると雪になってしまいますよ。
4. となりの小さい教室で勉強することになったよ。
5. 知らない漢字は書いてもらいました。
6. 安田さんには留学してほしいと思います。
7. 毎朝遅いけど元気ないんじゃないの？
8. 休みは一日パジャマのままです。

書いてみよう Contextualized writing

1. 今朝の天気は雨。朝に弱い私のクラスは昼からだけど、雪にはならないでほしい……。

2. 今日は休みだからサッカー部のみんなで晩ご飯にラーメンを作ってみました！たまごを入れるとすごくおいしい！

3. 安田先生
お元気でいらっしゃいますか？今留学で京都に来ていて毎日勉強がんばっています。まだ知らない漢字とかたくさんありますけど、日本が大好きです。日本語を教えてくださってありがとうございました！このポストカード、よかったら教室で使ってください。

知ってる? What do you know?

1	A	11	A	21	C
2	B	12	B	22	A
3	B	13	C	23	A
4	B	14	A	24	B
5	C	15	B	25	C
6	C	16	C	26	
7	A	17	B	27	
8	C	18	A	28	
9	B	19	C	29	
10	B	20	B	30	